cop. a

B   Fichman, Martin,
WALLACE   1944-

Alfred Russell
Wallace

B
WALLACE Fichman, Martin,
              1944-   *cop. a*

Alfred Russell
Wallace

1295

DATE	BORROWER'S NAME	

12 X 04 4/04

Twayne's English Authors Series

EDITOR OF THIS VOLUME

Herbert Sussman

Northeastern University

Alfred Russel Wallace

TEAS 305

Alfred Russel Wallace

ALFRED RUSSEL WALLACE

By MARTIN FICHMAN

Glendon College, York University, Toronto

eop. a

TWAYNE PUBLISHERS
A DIVISION OF G. K. HALL & CO., BOSTON

Published in 1981 by Twayne Publishers,
A Division of G. K. Hall & Co.
All Rights Reserved

Printed on permanent/durable acid-free paper and bound
in the United States of America

First Printing

Frontispiece photo of Alfred Russel Wallace,
Picture Collection,
The Branch Libraries,
The New York Public Library.

Library of Congress Cataloging in Publication Data

Fichman, Martin, 1944–
Alfred Russel Wallace.

(Twayne's English authors series ; TEAS 305)
Bibliography: pp. 174–82
Includes index.
1. Wallace, Alfred Russel, 1823–1913.
2. Natural selection.
3. Naturalists—England—Biography.
I. Title.   II. Series.
QH31.W2F52   574'.092'4 [B]   81–2566
ISBN 0–8057–6797–5   AACR2

To My Parents

Betty Fichman

and

Fred Fichman

Contents

About the Author

Born in Brooklyn, New York, in 1944, Martin Fichman received the B.Sc. degree from the Polytechnic Institute of New York and the A.M. and Ph.D. degrees from Harvard University and is currently associate professor of History and Natural Science at York University (Glendon College), Toronto. He has published articles on Alfred Russel Wallace and on the history of chemistry and is a contributor to the *Dictionary of Scientific Biography*. He is presently working on a study of the interrelation between biological and sociopolitical ideas in the writings of late nineteenth-century evolutionists.

Preface

Alfred Russel Wallace was among the most brilliant Victorian naturalists and codiscoverer of one of the principal scientific achievements of the nineteenth century, the theory of natural selection. Although his accomplishments were fully recognized by his contemporaries, his reputation diminished somewhat in this century. Paradoxically, this situation has arisen partly through Wallace's persistent efforts to equate evolution by natural selection with the name of Charles Darwin in the public mind. I have, therefore, critically analyzed Wallace's major theoretical advances in order to clarify his central role in the history of evolutionary biology. Given the multiplicity of his scientific interests, I have focused on one aspect—his biogeographical system—which best exemplifies the broad power of his evolutionary synthesis. This has necessitated, in a study of this length, omitting detailed treatments of certain other facets of Wallace's biology, notably his views on the causes and extent of variation, the mode of inheritance, interspecific sterility, instincts, and botanical issues generally.

I have as a parallel aim the analysis of the interrelation between Wallace's biological and sociopolitical ideas. The common cultural, philosophical, and linguistic context of scientific and so-called extrascientific factors in the Victorian evolutionary debates is now recognized as indisputable. No leading biologist was more explicit—and perhaps more vulnerable—than Wallace in the attempt to integrate the methodology and conclusions of the natural sciences with social, political, and moral concerns. In assessing his efforts to forge a comprehensive philosophy of man and nature, I have emphasized Wallace's commitment to land nationalization and to socialism, as these have received less attention than his debt to spiritualism.

I am grateful to my friend Frederick Kirchhoff for his criticism and advice in the preparation of this text. Alan Richardson provided a number of excellent suggestions for Chapter 3. I am also indebted to the librarians of the Linnean Society of London and of the archives of the Imperial College of Science and Technology for their assistance. Finally, I must thank Karen Woodvine for the speed, accuracy, and cheer with which she typed the manuscript for this book.

Portions of Chapter 3 appeared in the *Journal of the History of Biology* (10 [Spring 1977]: 45–63).

MARTIN FICHMAN

Glendon College,
York University, Toronto

Chronology

1823 Birth of Alfred Russel Wallace (8 January), son of Thomas Vere Wallace and Mary Anne Greenell, at Usk, Monmouthshire.

1828 Family moves to Hertford.

1836 Leaves Hertford Grammar School.

1837 Sent to London to live with his brother John (apprenticed to a master builder). Associates with London secularists and is introduced to Owenite social and political philosophy. Sent next to learn surveying with his brother William in Bedfordshire.

1843 Death of Thomas Vere Wallace (April).

1844 Gains teaching post at Leicester Collegiate School. Meets Henry Walter Bates, who introduces him to entomology. Reads Malthus's *An Essay on the Principle of Population.* First acquaintance with phrenology and mesmerism.

1845 Death of brother William in Neath. Takes over his surveying business and has first modest financial success.

1848 Leaves for South American expedition with Bates (26 April).

1852 Returns to London. Meets T. H. Huxley.

1853 *Palm Trees of the Amazon* and *A Narrative of Travels on the Amazon and Rio Negro.* Visits Switzerland.

1854 Meets Charles Darwin.

1854– Leaves England (March 1854) for Singapore and com-
1862 mencement of eight years of travel and exploration in the Malay Archipelago.

1855 "On the Law which has Regulated the Introduction of New Species" (his first explicit public statement of the doctrine of evolution).

1858 Writes (February) "On the Tendency of Varieties to Depart Indefinitely from the Original Type" (Wallace's discovery of the principle of natural selection). Paper read (1 July)—jointly with an extract from Darwin's unpublished manuscript on natural selection—before the Linnean Society of London.

1862 Returns to London. Visits Herbert Spencer. Associates with Charles Lyell.

1864 "The Origin of Human Races and the Antiquity of Man Deduced from the Theory of 'Natural Selection' " (Wallace's application of natural selection to man).

1866 "The Scientific Aspect of the Supernatural." Marries Annie Mitten.

1868 Awarded Royal Medal of the Royal Society for his "labours in practical and theoretical zoology."

1869 *The Malay Archipelago.*

1870 *Contributions to the Theory of Natural Selection.*

1871 Presidential Address (January) to Entomological Society.

1872 Moves to Grays, Essex.

1874 *Miracles and Modern Spiritualism.*

1876 *The Geographical Distribution of Animals.* President of Biological Section of the British Association for the Advancement of Science. Moves to Dorking.

1878 *Tropical Nature and Other Essays.* Moves to Croydon.

1880 *Island Life.*

1881 Awarded Civil Service Pension in recognition of his work in science. Elected president of newly formed Land Nationalization Society. Moves to Godalming.

1882 *Land Nationalisation.* Receives honorary LL.D. from the University of Dublin.

1885 *Bad Times.*

1886– Lecture tour of North America.
1887

1889 *Darwinism.* Receives honorary degree of D.C.L. from Oxford. Moves to Parkstone.

1890 "Human Selection," declaring himself a Socialist. Awarded the Darwin Medal of the Royal Society.

1893 Election to a Fellowship of the Royal Society.

1895 "The Method of Organic Evolution" (defending the theory of gradual variations against William Bateson's theory of discontinuous variations). Botanizing tour in Switzerland.

Chronology

1898   *The Wonderful Century.*
1900   *Studies, Scientific and Social.*
1902   Moves to Old Orchard, Broadstone.
1903   *Man's Place in the Universe.*
1905   *My Life.*
1908   Receives the Order of Merit. Awarded Copley Medal of the Royal Society and (first) Darwin-Wallace Medal of the Linnean Society of London.
1909   Delivers last public lecture on evolution at the Royal Institute (22 January).
1910   *The World of Life.*
1913   *Social Environment and Moral Progress* and *The Revolt of Democracy.* Dies (7 November) and is buried at Broadstone, Dorset.
1915   Memorial plaque unveiled at Westminster Abbey (1 November).

CHAPTER 1

Introduction

I Early Years (1823–1848)

ALFRED Russel Wallace was born in Usk, Monmouthshire, on 8 January 1823, the eighth child of Thomas Vere Wallace and Mary Anne Greenell. His father had earlier possessed a modest independent income, but a spasmodic business career and a series of ill-fated financial speculations had reduced the family fortunes to the point that the elder Wallace enjoyed "comparative freedom from worry about money matters, because these had reached such a pitch that nothing worse was to be expected."[1] Despite the difficult economic circumstances, Alfred Wallace enjoyed a happy childhood in the picturesque Welsh village of his birth.

The family moved to Hertford in 1828, where Wallace began his only formal education two years later. He regarded this experience as practically worthless, except for his learning sufficient Latin to be able later to understand the names and descriptions of species. He also acquired enough French to read and converse easily in it. Far more important were the family's home library and the collection of a proprietary town library of which Thomas Wallace had become librarian. These permitted the child to indulge his taste for extensive if eclectic reading by providing "almost any book that I had heard spoken of as celebrated or interesting" (ML, I, 75). Wallace's older brother John, a mechanically gifted boy, taught him to make those gadgets and toys which the family's straitened circumstances rarely enabled them to purchase. Wallace thus early developed the technical skills which were to prove indispensable in his travels as a naturalist in South America and the Malay

15

Archipelago and which were always a source of health and enjoyable occupation to him.

Having left Hertford Grammar School at Christmas 1836, Wallace was sent early in the next year to live in London, where John had become apprenticed to a master builder. Although he spent only a few months there, the period was an extremely significant one in his life. Aside from the obvious attractions of the capital, Wallace encountered advanced political and social ideas. He was taken regularly by his brother to evening meetings at a "Hall of Science"—Wallace termed it a "kind of club or mechanics' institute for advanced thinkers among workmen" (ML, I, 87)—in Tottenham Court Road, where the followers of Robert Owen lectured. The principles of Owenite social and political philosophy, though hardly appreciated fully by the thirteen-year-old, were later to shape Wallace's own reformist views. Whether these early working-class associations—a background quite different from that of Darwin, Lyell, Hooker, and most other early Victorian "gentlemen-naturalists"—account for his later somewhat atypical position within the British professional scientific community remains a moot question. There is little doubt that these contacts instilled in him a dedication to radical and egalitarian ideals which were to dominate his mature social and political thought.[2] In London, there were also lectures on agnosticism and secularism which, coupled with his reading of Thomas Paine's *The Age of Reason*, effectively challenged the elements of religion Wallace had imbibed from his orthodox but scarcely insistent Church of England parents. Wallace seems to have escaped the endemic Victorian crisis of belief, but the hold of secular rationalism upon him was to prove incomplete.

In the summer of 1837 Wallace went to join his brother William, a land-surveyor, in Bedfordshire to acquire the rudiments of surveying and mapping. William's work took them to various regions of England and Wales during the next several years. Late in 1841 they settled in Neath (in Glamorganshire, Wales) to survey and prepare corrected maps of the district. The work was not onerous and Wallace found ample time to savor the delights of the Welsh moors and mountains. His botanical pursuits were simply those of an interested amateur, characterized by his brother as worthless. Nevertheless, given his extreme ignorance of natural history any exposure to systemic study, including his acquisition of John Lindley's *Elements of Botany* and John C. Loudon's *Encyclopedia of Plants*, was beneficial. More crucial in Wallace's development as a naturalist than his own collection and identification of British specimens, however, was the delight the descriptions of exotic plants yielded. These produced in his mind a "weird and mysterious charm, which was extended even to [British] species, and which, I believe, had its share in producing that longing for the tropics which a few years later was satisfied in the equatorial forests of the Amazon" (ML, I, 195).

Due to a scarcity of surveying work, his brother could no longer provide for him and Wallace was forced to seek other employment. At the start of 1844, he applied, successfully, for a post at the Collegiate School at Leicester. He remained there for a year, teaching reading, writing, and arithmetic to the younger boys and surveying to the older ones. It was at Leicester that Wallace encountered two works which exerted decisive influences upon his career: Alexander von Humboldt's *Personal Narrative of Travels* (in South America) and Thomas Malthus's *Essay on the Principle of Population*. Humboldt's vivid description of the tropics of South America provoked an intense desire in Wallace to travel to those regions, a desire earlier whetted by his reading (probably in 1842) Darwin's *Voyage of the 'Beagle.'*[3] Both books, and especially Darwin's style of writing— "so free from all labour, affectation, or egotism, and yet so full of interest and original thought" (ML, I, 256)—could hardly have failed to affect Wallace deeply and immediately, given his developing passion for natural history. The impact of Malthus's *Essay*, on the other hand, was not to be fully realized until 1858, when it provided Wallace with a major clue to the problem of the origin of species. It was at Leicester, also, that Wallace met Henry Walter Bates, the entomologist and his future companion in the Amazon. Bates introduced Wallace, whose knowledge of natural history had been confined to botany, to beetle-collecting. Bates's extensive personal collection was all the more amazing to Wallace when he learned that "the great number and variety of beetles, their many strange forms and often beautiful markings or colouring, [had] almost all . . . been collected around Leicester" (ML, I, 237). Bates's friendship provided a more direct stimulus than either Darwin or von Humboldt and, equipped with collecting-bottle, pins, and a storage box, as well as James F. Stephens's *Manual of British Coleoptera, or Beetles,* Wallace accelerated his pursuit of biological knowledge.

The year 1844 was significant in yet one more respect. Wallace heard his first lectures on mesmerism and was thus exposed to a subject which, under the broader rubric of psychical research, was to become a serious, and controversial, field of enquiry for him. Wallace had earlier read George Combe's essay on *The Constitution of Man* (1828), whose admixture of phrenological and progressivist ideas seemed to be corroborated by the mesmeric experiments he witnessed at Leicester and later repeated upon his students. His growing interest in psychical phenomena at this time must be viewed alongside Wallace's disavowal of the doctrines of orthodox religion. The secular rationalism to which he had been exposed in London was reinforced by some lectures he had heard on David Friedrich Strauss's *Life of Jesus* (1835). Further evidence of an initial antipathy toward religious attitudes appears in Wallace's annotations to William Swainson's *Treatise on the Geography and Classification of Animals* (1835), a copy of which he purchased in September 1842. Wallace dismissed as ridiculous Swainson's attempt to reconcile scripture, geology, and zoology. He denied the doctrine of special creation and indicated clearly that, at this point, he saw nonteleological causation, not natural theology, as the sole path toward the elucidation of the problems of natural history.[4]

The unexpected death of William in February 1845 induced Wallace to leave Leicester and take over the small surveying and building business his brother had established at Neath. Aside from the design and construction of a local Mechanics' Institute, Wallace found the work unpleasant and determined to give it up as soon as alternative employment became available. He consoled himself, meanwhile, with entomological and botanical collecting and began to focus his attention on central questions of philosophical biology. Wallace read extensively in those works—Charles Lyell's *Principles of Geology, Vestiges of the Natural History of Creation* (by the then anonymous author Robert Chambers), James Cowles Prichard's *Researches into the Physical History of Man* (1813), William Lawrence's *Lectures on Comparative Anatomy, Physiology, Zoology, and the Natural History of Man,* and Darwin's *Voyage of the 'Beagle'* (for the second time)—which dealt, either explicitly or implicitly, with evolution, the origin of species, the geographical distribution of animals and plants, and the difference between species and varieties.

Wallace and Bates discussed the possibility of a journey to the tropics during the latter's visit to Neath in the summer of 1847. The publication of William H. Edwards's *Voyage Up the River Amazon, including a Residence at Pará* suggested the location. Edwards's provocative description of the beauty and grandeur of tropical vegetation coupled with his information that traveling and living expenses there were moderate, convinced Wallace (and Bates) that the Amazon Basin was the appropriate region for their expedition. They contacted Edward Doubleday of the British Museum, who assured them the whole of northern Brazil was comparatively unknown and a collection of novel species of insects, landshells, birds, and mammals would easily pay their expenses. The latter factor was essential, for Wallace and Bates, unlike either von Humboldt (a man of independent means) or Darwin and Huxley (both of whom were officially attached to naval surveys), were without financial support and had to rely upon the sale of their specimens—in effect, they were to be two of the earliest professional collectors.[5] After a further study of the principal holdings of South American animals and plants at the British Museum, arrangements with an agent (Samuel Stevens) to receive and sell their collections, and a fortuitous meeting with W. H. Edwards (who happened to be in London then and wrote letters of introduction for them), Wallace and Bates left England on 26 April 1848, destined for Pará.

II *Voyages and Explorations (1848–1862)*

Wallace and Bates reached Pará (now Belém), Brazil, on 28 May 1848. For the next two years, traveling together and

separately, the coexplorers collected in the regions surrounding
Pará, along the Tocantins River, and along the Amazon up
to Barra. At Barra (today Manaus), the point of convergence
of the Upper Amazon and the Rio Negro, the two decided to
separate permanently in March 1850. Bates continued to explore the Upper Amazon during the next eight years, recording
his experiences and discoveries in the *Naturalist on the River
Amazon* (1863), a classic of nineteenth-century travel writing.
Wallace went on to explore the Rio Negro, the relatively unknown Uaupés, and other northern tributaries. His journey,
at times dangerous, and his observations of the flora and fauna
—as well as the human inhabitants—of the Amazon region are
recounted in the *Narrative of Travels on the Amazon and
Rio Negro* (1853). Wallace's first accomplishments as a professional naturalist, however, and the force of the *Narrative,* were
diminished by the loss of the majority of his specimens (not
previously shipped to England) due to the burning at sea of
the cargo ship *Helen* aboard which he had embarked for home
in 1852. Rescued some 200 miles from Bermuda, with the
captain and crew, after ten days adrift in lifeboats, Wallace
reached London with his life and nascent reputation intact.
The loss of his collections was disheartening, nonetheless, and
Wallace later wrote: "How many times, when almost overcome
by the ague, had I crawled into the forest and been rewarded
by some unknown and beautiful species! . . . How many weary
days and weeks had I passed, upheld only by the fond hope of
bringing home many new and beautiful forms from those wild
regions. . . . And now everything was gone, and I had not one
specimen to illustrate the unknown lands I had trod, or to call
back the recollection of the wild scenes I had beheld!"[6]

The malaise was shortlived, and Wallace entered quickly into
the scientific activity of the capital. The South American specimens he had sent back to England secured him the acquaintance
of important members of the Zoological and Entomological
Societies of London, including Thomas Henry Huxley. While
preparing for publication the *Narrative* and *Palm Trees of the
Amazon* (also 1853), Wallace was making plans for another
major expedition. A study of the zoological collections at the
British Museum convinced him that the Malay Archipelago

offered the best prospects scientifically and financially. The Archipelago was known to house a rich fauna but, except for the island of Java, had not been systematically explored by naturalists. Moreover, the numerous Dutch settlements afforded facilities and at least minimal amenities for the European traveler. With the assistance of Sir Roderick Murchison, president of the Royal Geographical Society, Wallace secured free passage to Singapore, whence began his eight years (1854–1862) and 14,000 miles of exploration and residence within the Archipelago.

The Malaysian travels constitute the most significant period of Wallace's life. It was the observation of the varied Malay fauna, particularly the striking contrasts between the animal productions of the eastern and western halves of the Archipelago, which enabled Wallace to develop his evolutionary hypotheses and write the two essays—"On the Law Which Has Regulated the Introduction of New Species" (1855) and "On the Tendency of Varieties to Depart Indefinitely from the Original Type" (1858)—which established him, with Darwin, as codiscoverer of the theory of natural selection. It was his prolonged stays in the towns and remote villages of the Archipelago which augmented the knowledge of alternative cultures he had first experienced among the indigenous Amazonian tribes. For Wallace, this intimate contact with uncivilized man forced him to question the basic assumptions of Victorian society and ponder the significance of the differences between civilized and savage man.[7] It was the relatively harmonious mode of life, and particularly the absence of a developed system of private property, among the native Malayan peoples which recalled the Owenite teachings of his youth and rendered Wallace a more critical observer (and subject) of competitive industrial capitalism upon his return to England. Wallace was not blind to the pecuniary implications of his expedition and realized that at this period in his life he was likely to earn more in the Archipelago than he could as a land-surveyor in Great Britain. But a (doubly) candid reply to his brother-in-law's entreaty to return home (in 1859), and to the charge that he was merely an "enthusiast," indicates the dominant cast of Wallace's attitude toward wealth: "The majority of mankind are enthusiasts only in one thing—

in money-getting; and these call others enthusiasts as a term of reproach because they think there is something in the world better than money-getting. It strikes me that the power or capability of a man in getting rich is in an *inverse* proportion to his reflective powers and in *direct* proportion to his impudence. It is perhaps good to *be* rich, but not to *get* rich, or to be always trying to get rich, and few men are less fitted to get rich, if they did try, than myself" (ML, I, 368–69). These eight years of travel, finally, provided Wallace with the cultural, anthropological, and zoological materials for *The Malay Archipelago* (1869), a masterpiece of Victorian travel literature and one which was recognized internationally as a brilliant evocation of the naturalist's craft.

III   A London Life (1862–1871)

Upon returning to London in the spring of 1862, Wallace went initially to live with his sister and brother-in-law (Thomas Sims) and then leased a small house for himself and his mother in St. Mark's Crescent, Regent's Park. The remuneration from the sale of his Malay collections had far exceeded Wallace's expectations. Many of the bird and insect specimens were of great beauty and either wholly new or of extreme rarity in England, commanding high prices. Wallace's agent, Samuel Stevens, had invested the proceeds in India Railway stocks which yielded an annual income of £300. This, together with the projected income from his remaining private collections, freed Wallace, for the time, from any financial concerns (ML, II, 360–61). He devoted himself to the sorting and description of the thousands of insect and bird species he had brought back, contributing a number of scientific papers to various professional societies. In 1864 he read a major essay to the Linnean Society on the variation and geographical distribution of the Malayan Papilionidae (an extensive family of large and elegantly colored butterflies) in which he explained instances of polymorphism and mimicry on the principle of natural selection. He also wrote several important papers on physical and zoological geography and on anthropology—including the celebrated "Origin of Human Races, and the Antiquity of Man deduced from the Theory of 'Natural Selection'" (1864)—which established him as one of Britain's leading biologists.

Of the influential scientists with whom Wallace now associated, Sir Charles Lyell exerted the strongest influence. Wallace saw Lyell frequently and they spoke (and corresponded) at length on a wide variety of subjects, notably human evolution. It was at Lyell's evening receptions that Wallace met many well-known figures, including the physicist John Tyndall, the period's major historian of ideas W. E. H. Lecky, and the Duke of Argyll. Wallace also became more or less intimate with a number of scientific luminaries including Darwin, Joseph Dalton Hooker, Sir John Lubbock, Francis Galton, and Thomas Henry Huxley. One of the first celebrated Londoners Wallace had sought out was Herbert Spencer, whom he (and Bates) had visited to extract, unsuccessfully, a clue to the "great unsolved problem of the origin of life" (ML, II, 23). Despite their divergent positions on certain issues in both the natural and social sciences, Wallace and Spencer were united by a passionate dedication to evolution and to social reform. Wallace derived much amusement "from the often unexpected way in which [Spencer] would apply the principles of evolution to the commonest topics of conversation" (ML, II, 33). It was, furthermore, Spencer's phrase "survival of the fittest" that Wallace preferred to his and Darwin's own expression "natural selection" as being less subject to erroneous personification and a more direct, rather than metaphorical, expression of the process of evolution.[8]

In July 1865 Wallace attended his first séance. He quickly became convinced of the authenticity of the phenomena he witnessed and, shortly thereafter, of their spiritualist interpretation. He proceeded to read widely in the spiritualist literature and, in 1866, brought together a large body of supportive evidence in an article entitled "The Scientific Aspect of the Supernatural." Though Wallace failed to persuade some of his most valued colleagues, including Huxley, Darwin, Tyndall, and the physiologist William Benjamin Carpenter, to treat his new interest seriously, he became an assiduous attendant at numerous séances during the remaining years of his London residence. In the spring of 1866 Wallace, then forty-three, married the eighteen-year-old Annie Mitten, daughter of the botanist William Mitten. He continued to live in London until 1870, with the exception of one year with his wife's family at Hurstpierpoint, amidst whose tranquil surroundings he completed much of the *Malay Archipelago*. This period was a productive one, with essays on animal coloration (including mimicry and protective resemblance), the notorious review of Lyell's tenth edition of the *Principles of Geology* (in which Wallace announced publicly his new views on the origin of man), and *Contributions to the Theory of Natural Selection* (1870). Unsuccessful in his efforts to gain either the assistant secretaryship of the Royal Geographical Society (which went to Bates) or the directorship of the new art and natural history Museum at Bethnal Green (which opened under direct management from South Kensington), Wallace's financial position became problematical owing to a series of ill-fated investments (ML, II, 361–63). The enthusiastic reception accorded the *Malay Archipelago*, however, assured Wallace of the prospect of some livelihood as an author and, despite his initial disinclination, as a public lecturer on evolution.

IV   *Labors, Scientific and Social (1871–1885)*

Having lived in London for eight years, Wallace was desirous of a life in the country where he could devote more of his time to gardening and rural walks. He moved first to Barking (March 1870) and then to Grays, a village on the Thames twenty miles from London, in March 1872. Although the move to Grays had been undertaken partly in anticipation of the directorship of Bethnal Green, Wallace was able to have a modest house built there despite his failure to secure the museum position. To supplement his income from writing and the sale of his tropical collections, Wallace became an assistant examiner in physical geography in 1871. Wallace continued this work, requiring only three weeks' effort and yielding an income of about £60 per year, until 1897 (ML, II, 406). In addition to numerous reviews and articles—many of which appeared in *Nature*, the journal in whose foundation in 1869 Wallace took part (ML, II, 54)—the Presidential Address to the Biological Section of the British Association for the Advancement of Science at Glasgow (1876), and the collection of essays on *Tropical Nature* (1878), Wallace published his two major scientific works, *The Geographical Distribution of Animals* (1876) and *Island Life* (1880). In 1878 Epping Forest had been acquired for the public and Wallace, anxious for a regular source of income, applied for the superintendency. Although supported by the presidents of the several London natural history societies and other prominent scientists, he was again unsuccessful in his quest for a professional post. Largely through the efforts of Darwin, Huxley, and the Duke of Argyll, who lobbied the prime minister (Gladstone), Wallace was awarded a government pension of £200 in 1881 in recognition of his services to science and, thereby, finally relieved of financial insecurity (ARW, pp. 257–59).

Scientific concerns were accompanied by an increased interest in spiritualism. From 1871 onwards, after attending his first séance with the celebrated medium D.D. Home, Wallace became a vigorous controversialist in defense of spiritualist claims. The publication of *Miracles and Modern Spiritualism* in 1874 made his name well-known in spiritualist circles and secured his invitation to many séances conducted by prominent mediums. This public advocacy was conducted both in print, including the vigorous debate with Carpenter, and, on occasion, in court, where Wallace testified on behalf of mediums accused of fraud. During the 1876 BAAS meeting, Wallace's decision to allow the reading of a paper by William F. Barrett on experiments in thought-reading provoked a heated discussion which was dramatically reported in the press.[9] When the Society for Psychical Research was formed in 1882, Wallace became a member. He declined repeated invitations to assume its presidency and, except for a visit to the United States in 1886–1887, played an increasingly less active role in spiritualist affairs during the remainder of his life. There was no diminution in the force of his convictions, however, and the imprint of spiritualist ideas is unmistakable in his last writings.

Social and political questions assumed a more immediate role in Wallace's career at this time. He had been critical of certain of the axioms of British political economy at least as early as his return from the Malay Archipelago, but had restricted his meliorist activities to support of humanitarian causes and occasional comments in the anthropological writings. The bitter controversy over Irish landlordism, which intensified in 1879–1880, drew Wallace directly into the movement for land reform in Great Britain and Ireland. Aware of the ineffectualness of many of the proposals being put forward, Wallace became convinced that state ownership of some type was essential for removing the abuses of existing land-tenure systems. The publication of an article by him in the *Contemporary Review* (1880) advocating nationalization attracted immediate attention. The Land Nationalization Society, with a program based on his principles, was formed in 1881 with Wallace as its first president. *Land Nationalisation: Its Necessity and Its Aims* was published the following year. Wallace became increasingly outspoken and radical in his political and economic views, urging nationalization of the railways and joining in the growing agitation for redistribution of wealth and reform of capitalist-labor relations. Though not yet a declared Socialist, Wallace's leftist orientation informed his analysis of the persisting economic depression which had gripped Britain since 1873. *Bad Times,* appearing in 1885, cited excessive war expenditures, unfettered industrial speculation, and rural depopulation as among the dominant causes of England's socioeconomic difficulties and signaled the direction his criticisms of liberalism and bourgeois culture would take in the last decades of his life.

V   Statesman of Darwinism (1886–1913)

Toward the end of 1885 Wallace received an invitation from the Lowell Institute of Boston to deliver a series of lectures during the late autumn of the following year. The opportunity to proselytize on behalf of evolutionary theory, and the financial rewards an extended American tour would yield, were attractive, and Wallace left London on 9 October 1886, arriving in New York on 23 October. The Boston lectures—which included discussions of the origin and uses of the colors of animals and plants, mimicry and other protective resemblances, and biogeography—were highly successful and formed the basis for *Darwinism* (1889), Wallace's major exposition of the theory of natural selection and its applications. He spent the next year traveling across the continent, repeating the Lowell lectures with

equal success in major American cities and in Toronto and King-
ston in Canada. Wallace met many of the United States' most
distinguished scientists, including the botanist Asa Gray (his
and Darwin's foremost American supporter) and the geologist
James Dwight Dana, as well as a host of leading political, social, and intellectual figures. In addition to talking on scientific
subjects and observing at first hand the flora and fauna of North
America, Wallace spoke publicly on his sociopolitical views,
though these were "altogether too revolutionary for many of
my hearers" (ML, II, 129). He also made the acquaintance of
America's leading spiritualists and temporarily resumed frequent
attendance at séances. The single most lucrative lecture he gave
in North America was not, in fact, on evolutionary biology but
one on spiritualism, entitled "If a Man Die, Shall He Live
Again?" and delivered to an enthusiastic San Francisco audience
of over a thousand persons (ML, II, 160).

Returning to England in August 1887, Wallace set to work on
Darwinism. He intended it not only as a popular treatise, but as
an answer to three decades of criticism directed against the
theory of natural selection. In June 1889 he moved to Parkstone
and busied himself once again with gardening and rural life. The
following year, Wallace wrote an article on "Human Selection"
for the *Fortnightly Review*, which he considered "the most important contribution [he had] made to the science of sociology
and the cause of human progress" (ML, II, 209). It also contained his first public declaration as a Socialist, a position Wallace held—or hoped—to be voluntaristic rather than doctrinaire,
admitting that "compulsory socialism is to me a contradiction
in terms—as much as would be compulsory friendship" (ML,
II, 268). In the summer of 1893 Wallace (and his wife) visited
the Lake District for the first time, and was particularly impressed with the evidence for former glaciation its rounded rocks
and abundant moraines afforded. Two years later he went with
his father-in-law on a short botanizing tour in Switzerland, where
he had a further occasion to examine glacial phenomena in the
spectacular setting of the Alps.

The last years of Wallace's life were active ones. He moved
once more, to Broadstone in November 1902, as the region
around Parkstone had become built up sufficiently to destroy its

rural character. His new home, Old Orchard, and especially its large garden were to be a constant source of interest and delight to him. The final decade witnessed no diminution in literary output. In addition to articles on a variety of scientific and sociopolitical topics, Wallace published two major statements on biological philosophy, *Man's Place in the Universe* (1903) and *The World of Life* (1910)—in which a fully developed spiritualist teleology is given expression—his autobiography *My Life* (1905), and, at the age of ninety, his final pronouncements on industrial civilization, *Social Environment and Moral Progress* and *The Revolt of Democracy* (both 1913). By the summer of 1913 Wallace's health began to fail. He could no longer walk about his garden as before, but had some of the rarer Primulas and other plants brought to a small plot in front of the windows of his study so he might see them. Although his faculties remained intact, Wallace grew progressively weaker and, on 7 November 1913, died peacefully in his sleep. Three days later, he was buried in the small hillside cemetery of Broadstone.

CHAPTER 2

Natural Selection

THE joint discovery of the principle of natural selection by Wallace and Darwin is among the most celebrated episodes in the history of science. And although their paths to discovery were similar, there is no doubt that the two naturalists arrived independently at identical conclusions concerning the origin of species.[1] Wallace's travels to South America (1848–1852) and to the Malay Archipelago (1854–1862) provided him with a vast body of observational data by means of which he was able to translate his evolutionary speculations (first suggested in a letter to Bates in 1845) into the rigorous theory announced in 1858. When Wallace embarked for Pará (now Belém, Brazil) on 26 April 1848 he was an amateur naturalist desirous of pursuing his "favourite subject—the variations, arrangements, distribution, etc., of species" (ML, I, 257). When he returned to England from the Malay Archipelago fourteen years later, he was a biologist of established reputation.

I   A Narrative of Travels on the Amazon and Rio Negro (*1853*)

Wallace reached Pará on 28 May 1848 and remained in South America for four years. His experiences are recounted in *A Narrative of Travels on the Amazon and Rio Negro* (1853), in which he describes his journeys in chronological order and records his observations on the flora and fauna of the Amazon basin. Wallace's interest in the human inhabitants was no less keen, and much of the *Narrative* is devoted to a detailed account of the life and customs of the residents of the cities as well as of the native tribes which he encountered in traveling through the interior of the continent.

29

Despite the novelty of Pará, Wallace was at first disappointed: "The weather was not so hot, the people were not so peculiar, the vegetation was not so striking, as the glowing picture I had conjured up in my imagination, and had been brooding over during the tedium of a sea-voyage. . . . [D]uring the first week of our residence in Pará, though constantly in the forest in the neighbourhood of the city, I did not see a single humming-bird, parrot, or monkey" (N, pp. 3–4). The naturalist's trade had to be learned by patience and experience and one of the major achievements of the Amazon travels was Wallace's transformation from an amateur into a professional naturalist, fully capable of appreciating the various peculiarities of different regions —"the costume of the people, the strange forms of vegetation, and the novelty of the animal world" (N, p. 3). Indeed, after only two months of collecting at Pará, Wallace and Bates were able to send their first specimens back to England—a total of more than 1,300 species of insects (N, p. 34).

The coexplorers traveled together for two years, though each collected independently at various times in the environs of Pará, along the Tocantíns River, and up the Amazon as far as Barra (today Manaus). At Barra, where the Rio Negro joins the Amazon, the two decided to separate permanently in order to maximize their collections; Wallace went on to explore the Rio Negro, the relatively unknown Uaupés, and other northern tributaries, while Bates continued along the Upper Amazon. The journey up the Uaupés was one of the high-points of Wallace's South American sojourn. He wrote, nearly sixty years later, that, so far as he had heard, "no English traveller had to this day ascended the Uaupés River so far as I did, and no collector has stayed at any time at Javita, or has even passed through it" (ARW, pp. 23–24). The map which Wallace constructed, detailing not only the course and width of the river for its first 400 miles but also the location of the various Indian tribes inhabiting its banks as well as of the most important vegetable products of the surrounding forest, remained the most accurate one until the twentieth century.[2]

It was on the Uaupés that Wallace had his first encounter with "man in a state of nature—with absolute uncontaminated savages!" Unlike the half-civilized tribes among whom he had lived previously, the Uaupés Indians were in "every detail . . . original and self-sustaining as are the wild animals of the forests, absolutely independent of civilization, and who could and did live their own lives in their own way, as they had done for countless generations before America was discovered." The appearance and behavior of these Indians left an indelible impression on Wallace: "I could not have believed that there would be so much difference in the aspect of the same people in their native state and when living under European supervision. The true denizen of the Amazonian forests, like the forest itself, is unique and not to be forgotten" (ML, I, 288; N, pp. 190–94, 334–52).

Wallace's fascination with the Amazonian aborigines did not preclude a critical response to the culture of the half-civilized and urban inhabitants. In district after district, he noted that the "indolent disposition of the people . . . will prevent the capabilities of this fine country from being developed till European or North American colonies are formed" (N, p. 55). Despite Wallace's profound love of unspoiled nature, he shared (at this period in his life) the conviction of many of his contemporaries that nineteenth-century European civilization defined the standard by which all cultures should be measured. Thus his condemnation of the widespread practice of slavery in Brazil is chauvinistic as well as moralistic: "Can it be right to keep a number of our fellow creatures in a state of adult infancy,—of unthinking childhood? It is the responsibility and self-dependence of manhood that calls forth the highest powers and energies of our race. It is the struggle for existence, the 'battle of life,' which exercises the moral faculties and calls forth the latent sparks of genius. The hope of gain, the love of power, the desire of fame and approbation, excite to noble deeds, and call into action all those faculties which are the distinctive attributes of man" (N, p. 83).

A Narrative of Travels is significant as the first example of Wallace's interweaving of biological theory with personal narrative—a mode which would be so successfully exploited in *The Malay Archipelago* (1869)—rather than as a contribution to the scientific literature. The sinking of the ship Wallace had taken for his return voyage to England in 1852 resulted in the loss of his extensive private collection of insects and birds as well as the majority of his sketches, drawings, notes, and journals. That he was able to write the *Narrative*, the *Palm Trees of the Amazon and Their Uses* (1853), and several technical papers on the basis of the meager materials he salvaged from the burning vessel—careful sketches of the Amazonian species of palms and fishes, his diary while on the Rio Negro, some notes for maps of that river and the Uaupés, plus the letters he had sent home (ML, I, 305–306, 313–14)—is testimony to his growing skill as a naturalist. And despite the obvious shortcomings of the *Narrative* from the standpoint of precise data and documentation, Wallace did set forth certain observations and ideas on geographical distribution and speciation that were to be impressively developed in his later work.

The study of the geographical distribution of animals (and plants) was a familiar one at the time of Wallace's voyage to South America. Explanations of distributional data were, however, generally embedded within the framework of some version of the argument from design, an argument which received an influential (and ponderous) rendition in the 1830s with the publication of the eight *Bridgewater Treatises*.[3] Most naturalists believed that the multiplicity of species, their detailed—at times apparently perfect—adaptations to their particular environments, and the succession of organic forms in time were all the product of the wisdom and foresight of a Creator God. Although advances in geology and, to a lesser degree, biology had seriously eroded the authority of biblical interpretations in questions of natural history, some role for divine Providence in the course of nature was accepted—particularly in Great Britain where natural theology retained a strong influence—by many writers on biological and geological subjects.[4] Though few by the 1840s and early 1850s any longer held to the theory of special creation—namely, that species had been created directly by supernatural causation to fit particular environmental conditions—there was a consensus that the development of life was part of a harmonious and divinely inspired plan worked out through the agency of secondary (natural) causes.[5]

In the *Narrative*, then, Wallace was stating received opinion when he noted that "countries possessing a climate and soil very similar, may differ almost entirely in their productions. Thus

Europe and North America have scarcely an animal in common in the temperate zone; and South America contrasts equally with the opposite coast of Africa; while Australia differs almost entirely in its productions from districts under the same parallel of latitude in South Africa and South America" (N, p. 326). However, on the assumption that the characteristic fauna of a region was the direct "product" of environmental conditions, this dissimilarity of the faunas of ecologically identical areas was problematical. For those regions separated by great ocean or mountain barriers, it could plausibly be argued that the present faunas were (in some unspecified manner) the product of history as well as ecology. Thus, faunal differences would be expected and would have been maintained by water and land barriers to the dispersion and intermingling of species. But, as Wallace had discovered in his travels in the Amazon region, places "not more than fifty or a hundred miles apart often have species of insects and birds at the one, which are not found at the other" (N, p. 327). The existence of several closely related but not identical species in *adjacent* areas of practically identical climate and topography was unexpected.[6]

Wallace had been much struck by the fact that rivers, though generally easily passable by birds and insects, frequently acted as sharp demarcations between closely related species. The two beautiful butterflies *Callithea sapphira* and *C. Leprieuri*, collected by him along the Amazon, are each restricted to one bank though separated only by the expanse of the river. Three species of the genus *Psophia*, the Trumpeters, are also separated by river boundaries. The Common Trumpeter (*Psophia crepitans*), the widest ranging of the three species, is never found on the south bank of the Amazon. The Green-winged Trumpeter (*P. viridis*) is found only on the south bank of the Amazon and east of the Madeira River up to the forests of Pará. Finally, the White-winged Trumpeter (*P. leucoptera*) is also found on the south bank of the Amazon, but only west of the Madeira. A similar localization of the monkeys of the Amazon region emphasized the anomaly: there should not have been a number of slightly different species in a given ecological niche (N, pp. 328–29).

The recognition that the distribution of closely allied species was often marked by precise boundaries is the most important consequence of Wallace's travels in the Amazon Basin. Thereafter, he insisted upon the need to specify the exact locale at which species and varieties were collected. This rigor was not the practice of naturalists then—vague designations such as "Amazon" or even "South America" being frequent in the standard catalogues of species—and Wallace himself had not been entirely aware of the need for precise notation of locale when he began collecting (ML, I, 377). While he did not, in the *Narrative*, adduce this data on geographical distribution to support a theory of evolution, it is probable that he was fully aware of their significance in suggesting that closely allied species in adjacent areas resulted from an earlier isolation of populations from an original stock (for example, by chance migration across river barriers) with subsequent variation and formation of distinct species.[7] And in one passage Wallace explicitly controverted the hypothesis that adaptation to conditions was the determining factor in the distribution of species:

In all works on Natural History, we constantly find details of the marvellous adaptation of animals to their food, their habits, and the localities in which they are found. But naturalists are now beginning to look beyond this, and to see that there must be some other principle regulating the infinitely varied forms of animal life. It must strike every one, that the numbers of birds and insects of different groups, having scarcely any resemblance to each other, which yet feed on the same food and inhabit the same localities, cannot have been so differently constructed and adorned for that purpose alone. Thus the goat-suckers, the swallows, the tyrant fly-catchers, and the jacamars, all use the same kind of food, and procure it in the same manner: they all capture insects on the wing, yet how entirely different is the structure and the whole appearance of these birds! (N, p. 58)

Though no evolutionary explanation was posited, the *Narrative of Travels* signaled the direction Wallace's ideas were to take.

II   "On the Law Which Has Regulated the Introduction of New Species"

Although the solution to the problem of the origin of species still eluded him, Wallace returned from South America with a more sophisticated understanding of major issues in natural history. In London, from October 1852 onwards, he prepared the manuscripts for *A Narrative of Travels on the Amazon and Rio Negro* and *Palm Trees of the Amazon and Their Uses,* both of which were published in 1853. His South American collections had made Wallace's name known to the leading members of the Zoological and Entomological Societies (including Thomas Henry Huxley, later public advocate for evolution), and he attended meetings of both groups assiduously. Wallace read several brief papers on Amazonian butterflies, monkeys, and fishes, as well as one "On the Insects Used for Food by the Indians of the Amazon." During this period he also studied the extensive insect and bird collections of the British Museum and the Linnean Society and the botanical collections at the Kew Herbarium.

Committed to another voyage as the most certain means both of securing his reputation as a naturalist and of providing the data required for the elucidation of the species problem, Wallace decided upon an expedition to the Malay Archipelago. The collections in London indicated that the Archipelago was promisingly rich in the number and variety of its species; moreover, the fact that the natural history of the region (with the exception of the island of Java) had been relatively unexplored ensured that specimens of its lesser-known fauna would find a ready market in Europe. The journey to the East was too costly for Wallace's private resources, but through the intercession of Sir Roderick Murchison, then president of the Royal Geographical Society, Wallace gained free passage on the steamer *Euxine,* which left England in March 1854. Disembarking at Alexandria, he proceeded overland to Suez, where he boarded the steamer *Bengal* and arrived in Singapore on 20 April 1854 to "begin the eight years of wandering throughout the Malay Archipelago, which constituted the central and controlling incident" of his life. These eight years were to see Wallace travel nearly 14,000 miles, collect the vast sum of 125,660 specimens of natural history, and formulate those ideas which became the basis of evolutionary biology.[8]

Pledged to some form of evolutionary theory since 1845,

Wallace made his first public statement of this position in an essay entitled "On the Law which Has Regulated the Introduction of New Species." Written in February 1855 at Sarawak (in Borneo) and published later that year in the *Annals and Magazine of Natural History*, the essay skillfully weaves together facts from geology and from the geographic distribution of animals and plants to construct an hypothesis that explains those facts as a consequence of evolutionary change.

Wallace begins by arguing that most previous explanations of the present—and sometimes curious—distribution of animal and plants were unsatisfactory because they failed to take into account the past history of the earth and its inhabitants. He had been impressed with recent theories in geology, particularly the doctrine of the uniformitarians (including Charles Lyell) advocating an endless but gradual repetition of geological changes throughout time. Wallace considered it incontestable that during the earth's immense history its surface has undergone successive gradual transformations, with a corresponding gradual modification in the forms of organic life as they adapted to new environmental conditions. The present distribution patterns, therefore, must be the result of all previous changes, organic and inorganic. He was particularly concerned with analyzing more closely the spatial and temporal relationships between species and noted that whereas the larger groups, such as classes and orders, are generally spread over the whole earth, the smaller ones, such as families and genera, are frequently confined to more limited districts. Further, when genera themselves are widely spread, it is well-marked groups of species that are peculiar to each limited district. And, most significant, when "a group is confined to one district, and is rich in species, it is almost invariably the case that the most closely allied species are found in the same locality or in closely adjoining localities, and that *therefore the natural sequence of the species by affinity is also geographical.*"[9]

Wallace next argued that the distribution of animals and plants in time—the fossil record—reveals marked similarities to their present geographical distribution. Whereas many of the larger groups (and some smaller ones) extend through several geological periods, there are peculiar groups found in a particular geological period (or formation) and nowhere else. Moreover—just as closely related species in the Amazon Basin occupied adjacent regions—species or genera are more closely related to those occurring in the same geological epoch than they are to species or genera separated from them by longer periods of geological time. Finally, just as the same (or similar) species generally are never found in widely separated regions without also being found in intermediate locations, the geological record does not show any abrupt disjunctions in the fossil remains of a given species: "In other words, no group or species has come into existence twice." From these circumstances, Wallace concluded that *"every species has come into existence coincident both in space and time with a pre-existing closely allied species."*[10]

Wallace's law drew together a large body of hitherto unrelated facts and provided a compelling explanation for "the natural system of arrangement of organic beings, their geographical distribution, their geological sequence, the phænomena of representative and substituted groups in all their modifications, and the most singular peculiarities of anatomical structure."[11] The 1855 essay, despite its brevity, is among the most forceful statements of evolution prior to the publication in 1858 of the Darwin-Wallace papers announcing the principle of natural selection. The concept of evolution itself was hardly novel, with prefigurations having appeared among the cosmologies of the ancient Greek philosophers. By the mid-eighteenth century, authors such as Diderot, Buffon, and Maupertuis were advocating explicit versions of transformist doctrine, and, by the beginning of the nineteenth century, sufficient "evidence from the fields of biogeography, systematics, paleontology, comparative anatomy, and animal and plant breeding was already available . . . to have made it possible to develop" convincing arguments for evolution.[12] Yet, resistance to the concept—particularly among eminent men of science such as Lyell (initially), Richard Owen (the English comparative anatomist and paleontologist), and Georges Cuvier (the brilliant French zoologist and scientific administrator)—was entrenched, and the work of the two best-known proponents of evolution, the distinguished French botanist and zoologist Jean Baptiste de Lamarck and

Robert Chambers, was the object of intensive criticism and—in Chambers's case—ridicule among professional geologists and biologists.

This widespread resistance to evolutionary hypotheses in the early Victorian period arose only in part from the challenge they posed to biological orthodoxy. At stake were far broader questions—philosophical, religious, methodological—which created difficulties for a number of fundamental precepts of Western culture. In addition to the more obvious, and celebrated, threats to traditional conceptions of man, society, and God, evolutionary biology accentuated an already vigorous debate on complex issues such as the nature of theory formulation and justification, the degree of divine activity in nature, the distinction between supernatural and natural entities, and the appropriate roles of deduction and induction in science.[13] That Wallace was impressed with the speculations—if not the arguments—of Lamarck and Chambers sets him apart from most biologists of the period. It has been suggested, in fact, that Wallace's initial ready acceptance of Chambers's views derived from his belonging—in the 1840s—more "to the non-biologically educated public than he did to the world of the professional scientist."[14] Though the reasons for Wallace's early conversion to evolution are obscure, there is no question that he was from the first aware of the conspicuous errors which marred Chambers's *Vestiges of the Natural History of Creation* (1844) and of the inadequacies of Lamarck's theory. His own law, in contrast, was impeccable from a scientific standpoint and—precisely because it was derived from well-established data—raised the evolutionary debate to a new level of rigor.

The immediate stimulus for the essay had been the 1854 publication of the "polarity theory" by the British naturalist Edward Forbes. It was Forbes's contention that paleontological evidence—the abundance of fossils from both the earliest and most recent geological periods, coupled with a relative scarcity of fossils from intermediate periods—was consistent with a divinely ordained scheme of creation necessitating a maximum development of generic types at the opposite poles (in time) of the system of nature.[15] Wallace, who was "annoyed to see such an ideal absurdity put forth" when the facts could be explained simply on the basis of known geological and biological processes, intended his essay both as a refutation of Forbes and, also, as the occasion for a preliminary statement of his own ideas on evolution (ARW, p. 54; ML, I, 355). Arguing against Forbes, Wallace claimed that during periods of geological stability conditions would be favorable for the appearance and continued existence of new forms of life; conversely, periods of geological activity and changes of climate in a given region "would be highly unfavourable to the existence of individuals, might cause the extinction of many species, and would probably be equally unfavourable to the creation of new ones." The increase of the number of species during certain epochs and the decrease during others were thus explicable "without recourse to any causes but those we know to have existed, and to effects fairly deducible from them."[16]

A further objection to Forbes's polarity theory—and one which exemplifies Wallace's methodological position at this time—lay in Forbes's assumption that both the fossil record and human knowledge of it were tolerably complete. Wallace, like Darwin, never tired of stressing that the fossil record was incomplete. · Whole geological formations, with their fossil remains from vast periods of time, are buried beneath the oceans and therefore largely inacessible to human inquiry. And because knowledge of the entire series of the former inhabitants of the earth is necessarily fragmentary, all hypotheses which proceed from the contrary assumption were to Wallace scientifically unacceptable. Quite apart from Forbes's explicit rejection of the doctrine of evolution, his work repelled Wallace by its a prioristic speculation, and the 1855 essay was clearly directed against such tendencies in biological thought:

The hypothesis put forward in this paper depends in no degree upon the completeness of our knowledge of the former condition of the organic world, but takes what facts we have as fragments of a vast whole, and deduces from them something of the nature and proportions of that whole which we can never know in detail. It is founded upon isolated groups of facts, recognizes their isolation, and endeavours to deduce from them the nature of the intervening portions.[17]

Wallace's arguments are, of course, not merely "deductions"

from facts: he was working within a specific theoretical framework, so much so "that several naturalists had expressed regret that he was 'theorising,' when what 'was wanted was to collect more facts' " (ARW, p. 83). That framework, moreover, was not only evolutionary but secular. What is conspicuous in the 1855 essay, as well as in Wallace's private notebooks of the period, is the total rejection of the concepts of divine intervention and design in nature.[18] In contradistinction to the majority of British scientists, who still adhered to some form of natural theology, Wallace restricted his theory to secondary causation alone. The early exposure to secular philosophy, reinforced by his prolonged contact with non-European cultures, freed Wallace—at this period—from those religious scruples which then colored much of biological and geological reasoning. Wallace opposed not only creationists, but also those evolutionists who incorporated providential or teleological elements into their systems—though he was later to reverse himself on the latter point.[19]

Because the 1855 essay was "only the announcement of the theory, not its development" (ARW, p. 54), Wallace dealt only with certain applications of the law that "every species has come into existence coincident both in space and time with a pre-existing closely allied species." The observed affinities among animals (and plants) was an obvious consequence of the law, and Wallace indicated how a combination of two modes of evolutionary development would account for past and present relationships. A new species, having for its immediate "antitype" (or parent stock) a closely allied species existing at the time of its origin, might, in turn, give rise to a third species. If this process continued, with each new species giving rise to but one further species on its model, the resulting system of affinities would be represented by a simple and direct line of succession in time. If, however, one species gave rise, at different times, to two or more new species, the series of affinities would be represented by a forked or many-branched line. Both patterns were evident in the fossil record and Wallace described the resulting evolutionary network in the now familiar imagery of a "complicated branching of the lines of affinity, as intricate as the twigs of a gnarled oak or the vascular system of the human body."[20] The evolutionary system of natural affinities was not only complex; it was incomplete. Using an argument parallel to the one he had employed against Forbes, Wallace stressed the scientific superiority of evolutionary classification to other schemes—notably arbitrary arrangements which fixed a definite number for the divisions of each group—because it proceeded from the premise that the fossil record was imperfect. Since many species may have become extinct without leaving any trace in the fossil record, while the precise historical order of fossils was not always ascertainable by the paleontological techniques then available, he argued that it would be difficult—perhaps impossible—to arrive at a complete and unambiguous biological classification. Despite these reservations, the evolutionary hypothesis did offer a strictly naturalistic explanation of affinities and suggested fruitful avenues for future research.

Data drawn from the geographical distribution of animals and plants was (and remains) a cornerstone of evolutionary theory, and Wallace demonstrated how his law readily accounted for those facts. The more isolated a region is from other land masses, and the longer its geological isolation, the greater will be the number of species, genera, and families peculiar to it. Conversely, adjacent regions will be populated by identical or closely allied species and genera, as Wallace had observed with the butterflies, monkeys, and fishes of the Amazon.

But it was the more singular phenomena of biogeography which provided Wallace with his most striking evidence, and he seized upon—as did Darwin—the distributional anomalies of the Galápagos Islands. The fact that each of the islands contained groups of animals and plants peculiar to itself but closely related to those of the other islands, as well as to those of the nearest mainland portions of South America, was inexplicable on the theory of special creation. The contrary would have been expected, since that theory presumed that regions with identical environments, such as the Galápagos Islands, should be populated with identical forms, whereas regions with markedly different environments, such as the Galápagos and the nearest South American mainland, should be inhabited by dissimilar forms. To Wallace, the "question forces itself on every thinking mind—why are these things so?" And the solution was clear:

The Galápagos are a volcanic group of high antiquity, and have probably never been more closely connected with the continent than they
are at present. They must have been first peopled, like other newly-
formed islands, by the action of winds and currents, and at a period
sufficiently remote to have had the original species [from South
America] die out, and the modified prototypes only remain. In the
same way we can account for the separate islands having each their
peculiar species, either on the supposition that the same original
emigration peopled the whole of the islands with the same species
from which differently modified prototypes were created, or that the
islands were successively peopled from each other, but that new
species have been created in each on the plan of the pre-existing
ones.[21]

In like fashion, the distributions in regions separated by mountain ranges (according to their time of formation) or oceans
(according to their depth) become readily understandable.

On the question of whether the succession of species in time
had been from a lower, less specialized, to a higher, more
complex degree of organization, Wallace argued that "the admitted facts seem to show that there has been a general, but
not a detailed progression. Mollusca and Radiata existed before Vertebrata, and the progression from Fishes to Reptiles
and Mammalia, and also from the lower mammals to the higher,
is indisputable."[22] His law accounted not only for this development of higher from lower forms of life, but also for apparent
cases of retrogression in the fossil record. Thus, it is possible for
a certain group—such as an order of the phylum Mollusca—to
have reached a high level of specialization and complexity at
an early epoch; geological changes could then have caused the
extinction of the more specialized—and hence more vulnerable—
representatives of the order, while leaving as the sole members
of a once rich and varied group only some lower, less-specialized
species. These latter will then have served as the antitypes for
future species, which may never attain to the high degree of
development of the earlier Mollusca. The retrogression in the
fossil record is, therefore, only apparent; in actuality, there had
been a progression—although interrupted—of Mollusca and the
theory of organic evolution is not contradicted.[23]

Wallace adduced one final set of facts in support of his hypothesis—the phenomena of rudimentary organs. The minute limbs hidden beneath the skin in many of the snakelike lizards and the complete series of jointed finger-bones in the paddle of the whale were examples—familiar to students of comparative anatomy—of organs generally useless to the animals possessing them. Similar cases (abortive stamens, rudimentary floral envelopes, and undeveloped carpels) could be drawn from botany, and Wallace insisted that if "each species has been created independently, and without any necessary relations with pre-existing species, . . . these rudiments, these apparent imperfections" are inexplicable and meaningless.[24] If, however, new species must be closely related to the species from which they arose, these rudimentary organs are a necessary consequence of the gradualness of evolutionary change. Before "the higher Vertebrata were formed, for instance, many steps were required, and many organs had to undergo modifications from the rudimental condition in which only they had as yet existed. We still see remaining an antitypal sketch of a wing adapted for flight in the scaly flapper of the penguin, and limbs first concealed beneath the skin, and then weakly protruding from it, were the necessary gradations before others should be formed fully adapted for locomotion."[25] Although Wallace's argument is partly vitiated by his erroneous definition of "rudimentary" organs—they are actually vestigial structures, remnants of organs once useful to parent species but useless, and rendered abortive by the action of natural selection, in later species—his recognition that their occurrence in nature must be explained on the basis of known biological processes is fully consistent with the evolutionary law he is propounding.

The 1855 essay is a remarkable, if somewhat flawed, document. It constructs a powerful argument in support of the thesis that new species evolve (though Wallace did not yet employ the word) from closely related, preexisting species, but suggests no mechanism for such change. Yet Wallace had produced, from his own observations and insights as well as from the work of Darwin, Lyell, Chambers, Lamarck, and others, a major attack on creationism. Wallace's relation to Lyell is particularly revealing. Lyell's *Principles of Geology*, with its suggestive remarks on biogeography and the struggle for existence in nature, as well as a convincing demonstration of how geological changes could cause the extinction of certain species, was a fundamenal source for the 1855 essay. But on the crucial question of the origin of new species—"the most difficult, and at the same time the most interesting problem in the natural history of the earth"[26]—Lyell had explicitly rejected Lamarck's theory of transformism and invoked special creation.[27] Thus Wallace's "hope" that his efforts to deduce a law which determined, "to a certain degree, what species could and did appear at a given epoch, [would] be considered as one step in the right direction towards a complete solution" of the species question, is a direct challenge to Lyell and the major opponents of the theory of organic evolution.[28]

Wallace was, therefore, somewhat surprised at the lack of public response to the appearance of the essay, although he realized that the death of Forbes the year before had removed the one naturalist who would have been most likely to initiate a critical discussion of his ideas among British scientists. It was from Bates that he first received some notion of the impact his work was destined to have. "I was startled at first to see you already ripe for the enunciation of the theory," Bates wrote on 19 November 1856. "The idea is like truth itself, so simple and obvious that those who read and understand it will be struck by its simplicity; and yet it is perfectly original. The reasoning is close and clear, and although so brief an essay, it is quite complete, embraces the whole difficulty, and anticipates and annihilates all objections." Bates was prescient in his belief that, although few naturalists would then be "in a condition to comprehend and appreciate the paper," Wallace was assured, ultimately, of a "high and sound reputation" (ARW, pp. 52–53). Indeed, two men who were prepared to appreciate the contents and implications of the essay—Lyell and Darwin—read it shortly after it appeared and were to be deeply influenced by Wallace.

Both Lyell and Edward Blyth (a British naturalist living in India) had specifically drawn Darwin's attention to the essay, fully recognizing the significance of Wallace's arguments for evolution. Darwin later wrote (1 May 1857) to Wallace that he could plainly see "that we have thought much alike and to a certain extent have come to similar conclusions," adding that

he agreed "to the truth of almost every word of your paper."
He also mentioned that he had been working for twenty years
on the "question how and in what way do species and varieties
differ from each other," noting that he was preparing for publication a major work on that subject (ARW, pp. 107–109). It
was, of course, another essay by Wallace—the famed 1858 essay
announcing his independent discovery of the principle of natural
selection—that finally forced Darwin into publishing *On the
Origin of Species* in 1859. At this period, however, Wallace knew
only that two of the most eminent Victorian scientists were
following his work with the closest attention. In fact, Lyell
wrote some years later (4 April 1867), that he considered certain points "in regard to the bearing of the geological and
zoological evidence on geographical distribution and the origin
of species" to have been laid down in the 1855 essay more
clearly than he could find "in the work of Darwin itself" (ARW,
p. 280). Despite the dearth of immediate public recognition,
Wallace's essay had brought him to the center of the evolutionary debate.

III *Toward Solution of the Species Question*

From 1855 to 1858, Wallace sent to England several articles
which are mainly descriptive accounts of the fauna and flora of
the islands he visited in the Malay Archipelago. Three of these
essays, however, deal explicitly with the theoretical implications of the 1855 law and reflect the increasing certainty of his
evolutionary convictions.

"Attempts at a Natural Arrangement of Birds" (1856) develops
the contention that a natural system of affinities based on evolutionary relationships provides the only basis for arriving at
a valid classification schema. Drawing upon his extensive knowledge of the birds of South America and, now, of the Malay
Archipelago—knowledge gained not only from field observations but from the "constant habit of skinning" and preparing
recently killed specimens—Wallace proposed an arrangement
of the Passerine (Perching) order, based upon the concept
of a forked, or many-branched, line of descent from common
ancestors. He held that previous classifications were inadequate

or false because they imposed arbitrary divisions which forced "every bird . . . into one of them, [resulting in] the most incongruous and unnatural combinations" of genera and families. Wallace specifically attacked a modification of Cuvier's system, then current in England, which divided the Passeres into five groups according to outward resemblance (primarily beak formation): the Conirostres or cone-beaks (including finches), the Dentirostres or tooth-beaks (tanagers), the Tenuirostres or slender-beaks (hummingbirds, sun-birds), the Fissirostres or split-beaks (kingfishers, goatsuckers), and the Scansores or climbers (parrots, woodpeckers).[29]

This version of Cuvier's system, Wallace argued, was based upon the similarity (or analogy) of superficial traits which were misleading for the purposes of systematics because they often represented independent adaptation (of unrelated organisms) to similar habits and food supply rather than any genetic affinity.[30] In contrast, Wallace proposed a classification based upon a complex of structural traits—internal as well as external—which would reveal the actual (or natural) relationships among different species, genera, and families. Features such as the texture and arrangement of feathers, the form of nostrils, or the form and strength of the skull, for example, because less easily adaptable to external conditions afforded more significant taxonomic criteria for assessing affinities. Such an ensemble of characteristics—particularly if it appeared universally throughout a given group—was the strongest evidence for natural as opposed to artificial kinship. On these grounds, Wallace concluded that of the accepted divisions of Passeres only two, the Fissirostres and the Scansores, were valid. The other three were artificial and, because they ware based on either inadequate or superficial criteria, could provide no unambiguous method for assigning any particular Passerine species to a given division.[31]

Moreover, although Wallace retained the Fissirostres and the Scansores as natural rankings, he did not do so for the traditional reasons. It was not beak formation which characterized the Fissirostres, but the combination of very short and weak legs, long (or, in any event, powerful) wings, and particular details of anatomical structure and plumage. The form of bill, so often used for taxonomic purposes, was clearly insignificant: among the

true Fissirostres (Wallace added certain species not before regarded as members of that division, while removing others so
placed on the basis of single traits alone), *every* form of bill—
conical, toothed, hooked, serrated, spear-shaped, curved, flat—
was found.[32] Similarly, the Scansores, which included the woodpeckers, cuckoos, parrots, and toucans, were ranked as a natural
group because of their short, rounded, very weak wings (incapable of rapid or prolonged flight), their large and powerful
feet (with the outer toe either turned completely backwards
or nearly at right angles to the rest), the particular form of their
sternum, and other anatomical details. Beak form was shown
once more to be irrelevant to classification as there are numerous and major variations in the form of beak and tongue among
the true Scansores.[33]

Although Wallace was later to amend details of his classification slightly, the 1856 essay exemplified the explanatory potential
of evolutionary theory. Not only had he successfully applied the
developmental hypothesis to a troublesome ornithological problem, but he had also clarified the question of what constituted
an evolutionary transition. The swallows and goatsuckers, considered by some to be connecting links between the Fissirostres
and other tribes or orders of birds, exhibited the most extreme
development of the Fissirostral characteristics. In them, "the
power of capturing insects on the wing has reached its maximum.
The gape is enormously wide, the feet generally very short, and
the wings long and powerful." Because they were the most highly
developed members of the group, however, Wallace argued that
they "must be most distinctly separated from all the species of
any other group" and could not possibly be transitional forms.[34]
By implication, it was clear that transitions between groups must
be sought among the least-developed forms: the common ancestor in the network of branching affinities.

Wallace continued to refine his evolutionary approach in a
"Note on the Theory of Permanent and Geographical Varieties"
(published in the *Zoologist* in 1858), which focused on the vexing question of the difference between species and varieties. The
conventional view—both biological and theological—held that
species were "absolute independent creations, which during their
whole existence never vary from one to another, while varieties

are not independent creations, but are or have been produced by ordinary generation from a parent species."[35] This definition, though apparently unambiguous, breaks down in practice, and Wallace exploited the dilemma by showing the logical inconsistency of the doctrine of "permanent varieties."

Species could be distinguished from varieties on two grounds. Using a quantitative criterion, any form whose characteristics differed from those of a given species, but within a specified limit, would be classed as a variety; any form whose differences exceeded the stated range of variation would be classed as a separate species. Alternatively, the difference between species and varieties could be regarded as qualitative "by considering the permanence, not the amount, of the variation from its nearest allies, to constitute the specific character." Thus, a species would be defined by the permanence of its distinguishing characteristics, whereas a variety would be unstable and might revert back to its parent form. Wallace asserted that neither definition was satisfactory. If species differed from varieties in degree only, the line that separates the two would be entirely arbitrary and "so fine that it will be exceedingly difficult to prove its existence."[36] Moreover, if the only difference between species and varieties was quantitative, "that fact is one of the strongest arguments against the independent creation of species, for why should a special act of creation be required to call into existence an organism differing only in degree from another which has been produced by existing laws?"[37] The criterion of permanence fared little better. Certain forms, the so-called "geographical varieties," were regarded as possessing characteristics which, though permanent, were not sufficiently distinct to allow their being classed as separate species. Such varieties shared the character of permanence with true species though, by definition, they were not special creations and Wallace remarked that it was indeed "strange that such widely different origins should produce such identical results." The conclusion was obvious: "the two doctrines, of 'permanent varieties' and of 'specially created unvarying species,' are inconsistent with each other."[38]

Although Wallace had begun the "Note" somewhat disingenuously by stating that he was not "advocating either side of the question," his position is evident from an examination of one of his private notebooks which he kept during the course of his travels in the Malay Archipelago. This notebook, containing entries from 1855 to 1859, is indispensable for a full understanding of the development of Wallace's ideas and was probably intended as the draft of an extensive book on evolution, about which he wrote to Darwin late in 1857 and to Bates early in 1858.[39] The entries dealing with the difference between species and varieties are of the utmost interest and indicate that at least as early as 1855 Wallace had concluded that there was no difference *in kind* between the two. His comments on the orthodox view that species can vary only within fixed, narrow limits are direct:

Lyell says that varieties of some species may differ more than other species do from each other without shaking our confidence in the reality of species — But why should we have that confidence? Is it not a nice prepossession or prejudice like that in favour of the stability of the earth which he has so ably argued against? In fact, what positive evidence have we that species only vary within certain limits? . . . We have no proof how the varieties of dogs were produced. All varieties we know of are produced at *birth*, the offspring differing from the parent. This offspring propagates its kind. Who can declare that it shall not produce a variety, which process continued at intervals will account for all the facts?[40]

The point of the "Note" now becomes clear. Convinced that there was no difference in nature between the origin of species and of varieties, Wallace sought to discredit the concept of species, as fixed, special creations by showing the inconsistencies which followed from such a definition. He was not able to offer an entirely satisfactory definition of his own—the definition of species was, and remains, a refractory problem—but he did demonstrate effectively that there was no *essential* difference between species and varieties and thereby removed one of the major obstacles to the acceptance of evolutionary theory.[41]

Despite the lack of any adequate mechanism for evolution, Wallace was interpreting the data from the Malay Archipelago with increasing mastery. His collecting in the Aru Islands (situated to the southwest of New Guinea and never before visited by an English naturalist)—which he regarded as the most successful of the entire travels (ML, I, 357)—provided the material for an essay "On the Natural History of the Aru Islands" (1857). The most striking characteristic of these islands was the absence of many widely distributed species of the western half of the Malay Archipelago (including Borneo, Sumatra, and Java) coupled with similarity—in many cases identity—between Aru species of birds, insects, and mammals (the groups Wallace collected most extensively) and those of New Guinea and, to a lesser degree, Australia. Using that combination of biological and geological reasoning which he had fashioned into a potent methodological tool, Wallace explained the anomalous distribution patterns of the Aru fauna on the basis of the evolutionary hypothesis and further eroded the special creationist position.

Given the wide interval of sea separating the Aru Islands from the coast of New Guinea—the average distance being 150 miles —the close resemblance of species was puzzling. The island of Ceylon, for example, is closer to the mainland of India than Aru is to New Guinea, yet Ceylon presents a fauna clearly distinct from its neighbor, including many unique species and, even, unique genera. Sardinia, about as far from Italy as Aru is from New Guinea, also presents a distinct fauna. Almost the only islands which did possess a rich fauna, nearly identical to their adjacent mainlands, were Great Britain and Sicily, and that circumstance, Wallace noted, "is held to prove that they have been once a portion of such continents, and geological evidence shows that the separation had taken place at no distant period." Arguing by analogy, Wallace declared that Aru must once have formed part of New Guinea and corroborated this by the fact that the Molucca sea, which bordered Aru to the West, was of great depth, whereas the sea eastward from Aru to New Guinea and southward to Australia was comparatively shallow. The shallow sea indicated a (geologically)recent land-connection which would have provided a common set of ancestors for the present-day faunas of the now-separate land masses.[42]

The distributional anomalies of the Aru Islands were of more than merely local significance: they reflected the broader historical changes of the entire Malay Archipelago and afforded Wallace new evidence against special creation. To account for the origin of new species, most naturalists—Lyell preeminent among them— held that as "ancient species became extinct, new ones were created in each country or district, adapted to the physical conditions of that district." Wallace emphasized that, according to Lyell, because extinction generally implied a change in physical conditions (to which existing species were ill-adapted), the new species would be *"perfectly dissimilar in their forms, habits, and organization"* to those species they replaced. This theory implied that regions possessing similar climate and topography would sustain similar fauna, while regions differing markedly in those respects would differ markedly in their animal populations. If special creation was the law which governed the introduction of species, there could be no contradictions to it, or at the very least, no striking exceptions. But the Malay Archipelago yielded Wallace the precise contradiction he had been seeking:

Now we have seen how totally the productions of New Guinea [and Aru] differ from those of the Western Islands of the Archipelago, say Borneo, as the type of the rest, and as almost exactly equal in area to New Guinea. This difference, it must well be remarked, is not one of species, but of genera, families, and whole orders. Yet it would be difficult to point out two countries more exactly resembling each other in climate and physical features. . . . If, on the other hand, we compare Australia with New Guinea, we can scarcely find a stronger contrast than in their physical conditions: the one near the equator, the other near and beyond the tropics; the one enjoying perpetual moisture, the other with alternations of excessive drought; the one a vast ever-verdant forest, the other dry open woods, downs, or deserts. Yet the faunas of the two, though mostly distinct in species, are strikingly similar in character.

Every family of birds (except one) found in Australia also is found in New Guinea; more important, many of the Australian genera are also found in New Guinea. Similar distribution chararterizes mammalian and insect groups. Wallace cited the presence of the kangaroo—perfectly adapted to the dry plains and open woods of Australia—in the dense and damp forests of New Guinea (but not of Borneo) as inexplicable on the creationist hypothesis. Similarly, the abundance of monkeys in Borneo—suited to its physical environment—was in direct contradiction to their total absence in New Guinea, whose physical conditions were practically identical. Some law other than special creation,

Wallace asserted, "has regulated the distribution of existing species . . . or we should not see countries the most opposite in character with similar productions, while others almost exactly alike as respects climate and general aspect, yet differ totally in their forms of organic life."[43]

The "other" law is Wallace's own, announced in 1855. Applied to the present case, the creationist contradictions disappear and the apparent distributional anomalies are resolved. At that period in the past when New Guinea and Australia were united, they shared a similar climate and physical geography and housed related or identical species. When the land masses separated, the climate of both regions would likely have been modified significantly, resulting in the extinction of many species. Subsequently, "new species have been gradually introduced into each [region], but in each closely allied to the pre-existing species, many of which were at first common to the two countries." This process would account for the present similarity (but not identity) between the fauna of New Guinea and Australia. Further, those groups absent from one—such as the monkeys from Australia—would "necessarily be so from the other also, for however much they might be *adapted* to the country [New Guinea], the law of close affinity would not allow of their appearance, except by a long succession of steps occupying an immense geological interval."[44]

Wallace continued the argument with respect to Aru to demonstrate the universal applicability of the 1855 law. Had the Aru Islands been separated from New Guinea for a longer period than was actually the case, the two faunas would be more distinct, though still related. The longer the hypothesized separation, the greater would have been the process of organic change, with some species having become "extinct in the one country, and unreplaced, while in the other a numerous series of modified species may have been introduced. Then the faunas will come to differ not in species only, but in generic groups. There would then be the resemblance between them that there is between the West India Islands and Mexico." If, finally, the separation of Aru from New Guinea had taken place at a period as remote as that when Madagascar separated from Africa, the Aru fauna would show "an exact counterpart of what we see now in Madagascar." There, although a general resemblance to African forms persists, the long-continued divergence of Malagasy species from the ancestral stock has resulted in many peculiar genera and even entire families.[45]

Wallace now had vindicated his theoretical propositions of 1855 by a cogent explanation of distributional data collected in the Aru Islands. He had, furthermore, shown the special creationist argument to be both redundant—"centres of creation," which had been advocated by certain naturalists, were unnecessary unless one literally invoked a "centre" in *every* island or district which possessed a unique species—and false—new species had *never* been created "perfectly dissimilar in forms, habits, and organization" from those which had preceded them.[46] Most significantly, he had indicated that anthropological data were as crucial to evolutionary theory as those drawn from the distribution of animals and plants. He alluded to the great interest with which he studied the physical and moral traits of the Papuans (natives of New Guinea, Aru, and the Kei Islands) and "noted the very striking differences that exist between them and the Malays, not only in outward features, but in their character and habits."[47] When Wallace later proposed (see Chapter 3) a definite boundary—"Wallace's Line"—dividing the flora and fauna of the eastern ("Australian") half of the Malay Archipelago from that of the western ("Indian") half, he proposed a similar (but not identical) boundary between the Malayan and Papuan types of men. Anthropological data had, however, at this time a more catalytic effect upon Wallace's thinking. It was the question of human evolution and the argument of Thomas Malthus's *Essay on the Principle of Population* (1798) that provided a direct clue to his discovery of natural selection.

IV *Discovery of Natural Selection*

Although the exact nature of Malthus's influence continues to be the subject of debate, it is clear that *An Essay on the Principle of Population* provided both Wallace and Darwin with a critical insight which enabled each of them to solve the question of *how* species originate. Wallace's autobiographical rendition of his moment of discovery provides a dramatic, if remote (it was written nearly half a century after the event) and somewhat uncritical, statement of scientific creativity. During an illness on the island of Ternate,[48] in late February 1858, Wallace, pondering those subjects which had most engaged him during his Malaysian travels, recalled the work of Malthus which he had read some twelve years before. Specifically, it was Malthus's vivid demonstration of "the positive checks to increase"—disease, war, accidents, and famine—which keep the population of savage races down to a much lower average than civilized races, which sparked Wallace's chain of reasoning:

It then occurred to me that these causes or their equivalents are continually acting in the case of animals also; and as animals usually breed much more rapidly than does mankind, the destruction every year from these causes must be enormous in order to keep down the numbers of each species, since they evidently do not increase regularly from year to year, as otherwise the world would long ago have been densely crowded with those that breed most quickly. Vaguely thinking over the enormous and constant destruction which this implied, it occurred to me to ask the question, Why do some die and some live? And the answer was clearly, that on the whole the best fitted live. From the effects of disease the most healthy escaped; from enemies, the strongest, the swiftest, or the most cunning. . . . Then it suddenly flashed upon me that this self-acting process would necessarily *improve the race*, because in every generation the inferior would inevitably be killed off and the superior would remain—that is, *the fittest would survive.*

It at once became clear to Wallace that natural selection (though he did not yet use that term) was the mechanism he had been seeking. Combining Lyell's description of the gradual fluctuations of land and sea, of climate, of food supply, and of predators, with his own field experience of organic variation in nature, Wallace realized that—given sufficient time—new species would evolve in response to altered environmental conditions. The exquisite and often complex adaptations of animals were now explicable, not as the product of design, but as the outcome of evolutionary change (ML, I, 360–62).

Upon recovery, Wallace wrote out his theory as an essay entitled "On the Tendency of Varieties to Depart Indefinitely from the Original Type," and mailed it to Darwin with the request that he show it to Lyell, "should he think it sufficiently novel and interesting."[49] Wallace, although aware that Darwin was preparing for publication his great work on species and varieties, did not know that the latter, too, had discovered natural selection but had not yet published on it. Darwin, on the contrary, had probably discerned Wallace's progress on the species question from his letters as well as the pre-1858 articles, and was stunned— but not surprised—to receive Wallace's sketch whose "terms now stand as heads of my chapters."[50] As Lyell had warned, Darwin was forestalled and he was tormented over the proper course of action. Wallace had not specifically instructed Darwin to publish the essay, but the latter realized that publication was the only honorable step. Fortunately for Darwin, his close friends Lyell and Joseph Dalton Hooker arranged a compromise by which both he and Wallace were accorded priority: on 1 July 1858, Wallace's essay was read before the Linnean Society, preceded by extracts from an unpublished essay on natural selection written by Darwin in 1844 and from a copy of a letter from Darwin to Asa Gray (dated 5 September 1857) which discusses the "princi-ple of divergence"—an important part of the theory not dis-cussed in the 1844 manuscript.[51]

Wallace, in distant Malaysia, was ignorant of the distress his essay had caused Darwin and of the skillful manner in which Lyell and Hooker had extricated Darwin from his dilemma. He never questioned the propriety of the joint publication—indeed, he wrote home that Darwin had shown his essay to "Dr. Hooker and Sir C. Lyell, who thought so highly of it that they immedi-ately read it before the Linnean Society," thus ensuring Wallace "the acquaintance and assistance of these eminent men on [his] return home"—and went so far as to assure Darwin that he con-sidered the theory of natural selection to be Darwin's and Dar-win's only (ARW, pp. 57, 131). Wallace's persistent deference— public and private—to Darwin was generous, but curious in the extreme. Although he later issued statements establishing the independence of his discovery and emphasized that his essay had been printed without his knowledge, "and of course without any correction of proofs,"[52] it is primarily Wallace's own doing that the theory of evolution by natural selection is not infrequently known as Darwinism. In fact, there were significant differences between his and Darwin's formulations of the theory—differences which, as we shall see, intensified through the years. But in 1858 the relatively unknown Wallace could well be satisfied with having his name indelibly associated with that of a member of Britain's scientific elite.

The object of Wallace's 1858 essay was to show "that there is a general principle in nature which will cause many *varieties* to survive the parent species, and to give rise to successive variations departing further and further from the original type."[53] The argument proceeds from the premise that the "struggle for existence" among animals in the wild (necessitated by the disparity between the immense number of animals born and the limited resources necessary to sustain life) leads ineluctably to the survival of those individuals (within a given species) which are best equipped to meet and overcome the checks imposed by the precariousness of the food supply, the constant predations of enemies, and the vicissitudes of the seasons. Analogously, among the several allied species of a group, those which are best adapted to surrounding conditions will increase at the expense of other species, which themselves diminish in population and, in extreme cases, become extinct (NS, pp. 23–26). Turning to the central issue of the relation between varieties and species, Wallace noted that variations from the typical form of a species must have some definite effect, however slight, upon the habits or capacities of the individuals possessing them. Changes such as difference in color (by rendering the animal more or less conspicuous and thus affecting its safety) or alteration in the strength or dimension of limbs or other external organs (by rendering the animal more or less capable of procuring food), for example, would affect the survival power of the variant. Those varieties possessing useful variations will tend to increase in numbers, and keep their numerical superiority, while those possessing useless or harmful variations will tend to diminish.

If, now, in a district populated by a parent species plus varieties some alteration of environmental conditions (such as drought or invasion of new predators) occurred which rendered existence more difficult, those individuals which formed the least numerous and feeblest variety would suffer first and, under continued environmental pressure, become extinct. If the altered conditions persisted, the same fate might meet the parent species, leaving only the superior variety. This last could never revert to the parent form because it would be a more adapted organism and the parent species could not compete successfully with it for existence. But this new, improved, and populous race might itself, in time, give rise to new varieties which, by the same general law, become predominant and replace their parent forms completely. If the process of "progression and continued divergence" continued through a sufficiently vast period of time, the ultimate variety will have departed far enough from the original type to be classed as a separate species. The origin of new species, therefore, is (in part) the result of the struggle for existence between closely related members of a population and the fact that variations among those members do frequently occur in nature (NS, pp. 27–29).

One of the strongest arguments which had been brought forward to prove the fixity of species was that varieties produced under domestication are unstable and, left to themselves, generally revert to the normal form of the parent species. This instability was thought to characterize, also, varieties occurring among wild animals, causing them to either revert to the parent form, or at most, vary within strictly defined limits. Wallace contended that the analogy was invalid—his essay proves just the opposite with respect to wild varieties—and, moreover, that the partial reversion of domestic varieties follows directly from the principle of natural selection. Domestic animals are artificial in that they are protected by man and thereby removed from the rigors of the struggle for existence. Variations which arise among them are selected and bred according to human requirements and, often, those which would render a wild animal unable to compete with its fellows are no disadvantage whatever in a state of domesticity. Short-legged sheep, pouter pigeons, and poodle dogs "could never have come into existence in a state of nature, because the very first steps towards such inferior forms would have led to the rapid extinction of the race; still less could they now exist in competition with their wild allies" (NS, p. 31). If domestic animals were turned wild they would either become extinct or vary in a direction which would again adapt them to existence in the wild—that is, they would of necessity return to something approximating the original species.

Natural selection also accounted for a series of puzzling facts which hitherto had resisted adequate scientific explanation. The multiple lines of divergence from an ancestral form required no metaphysical or providential rationale but followed directly from naturalistic processes. The "increasing efficiency and power of a particular organ through a succession of allied species"—the result of continued selective pressure—as well as the "remarkable persistence of unimportant parts," such as the form of horns or crests and the texture of plumage, "through a series of species differing considerably" in other characters—"unimportant" parts being subject to little or no selective pressure—are necessary consequences of Wallace's theory. The latter point was of particular interest as it provided a rigorous basis for the evolutionary systematics he had suggested in the essay on the natural classification of birds. Wallace's terse conclusion encapsulates his achievements and testifies to his conviction, at this time, that evolution is nonteleological:

[T]here is a tendency in nature to the continued progression of certain classes of *varieties* further and further from the original type—a progression to which there appears no reason to assign any definite limits. . . . This progression, by minute steps, in various directions, but always checked and balanced by the necessary conditions, subject to which alone existence can be preserved, may, it is believed, be followed out so as to agree with all the phenomena presented by organised beings, their extinction and succession in past ages, and all the extraordinary modifications of form, instinct, and habits which they exhibit (NS, p. 33).

The joint publication marked a turning point in the history of biology, though it seems to have generated minimal public response at the time. Wallace's essay was the more impressive contribution—as Darwin himself noted (ARW, p. 112)—despite the fact that he had not intended it for publication in that form. And though Darwin assured Wallace that his "share in the theory will [not] be overlooked by the real judges, as Hooker, Lyell, Asa Gray, etc.," it was to Darwin that full public recognition came with the publication of *On the Origin of Species* (1859) the following year (ARW, pp. 112, 115). Wallace recognized that

Darwin's book, brilliantly written with a wealth of illustrative examples, would advance the evolutionary cause among the general public as well as the scientific community, and in recommending it to his friend George Silk declared that "Mr. Darwin has given the world a *new science,* and his name should, in my opinion, stand above that of every philosopher of ancient or modern times. The force of admiration can no further go!!!" (ML, I, 372–73).

Actually, there were limits to Wallace's admiration. Darwin relied heavily upon the analogy between human selection and natural selection in presenting the case for evolution, whereas Wallace considered that analogy suspect and misleading (NS, p. 31). He held it to be a major weakness that Darwin utilized so extensively the evidence of variation and selection among domestic animals and plants, and devoted his own career toward demonstrating that the theory of evolution could be supported solely by the evidence of variation in the wild. Darwin's use of data from artificial selection, however, did clarify the concept of variation by showing that natural selection acted both upon individual differences (to produce varieties) and, secondarily, upon differences between varieties (to produce species)—a distinction which was not entirely clear in Wallace's essay.[54] The Lamarckian notion of the inheritance of acquired characters was a further source of contention between the two naturalists, and Darwin's occasional endorsement of that hypothesis seemed to Wallace to seriously weaken the strict theory of natural selection.[55] In 1858, however, the differences between Darwin and Wallace were far less significant than the fact of their joint discovery. Catapulted to the forefront of Victorian science, Wallace could devote the remainder of his Malaysian travels—the valetudinarian Darwin was "astonished" to learn that Wallace expected to remain away from England for three or four more years (ARW, p. 110)—toward gathering that additional evidence necessary to support the theory against the anticipated hostility of its critics.

CHAPTER 3

Biogeography

WALLACE'S major achievements in science were in the field of biogeography, particularly the geographical distribution of animals (zoogeography). Since antiquity, naturalists had been aware that different regions generally housed distinct and characteristic fauna and flora, the differences assumed to be due solely to varied climates and physical conditions. It was Buffon who, in the mid-eighteenth century, definitively challenged the adequacy of the traditional explanation by pointing out that the tropical regions of the Old and New World—regions of practically identical ecology—differed strikingly in their indigenous mammals. By 1820 Buffon's observation had been broadened—particularly by Humboldt and the Swiss botanist A-P de Candolle—to include most other animals and plants. Naturalists now recognized that any regions, even of identical ecology, separated by barriers (such as mountains or oceans) would have distinct and characteristic organic productions. Most important, it was understood that the present distributional patterns of animals and plants were determined by historical factors (past changes both organic and geological) as well as by existing ecological conditions.[1] Wallace, in a series of articles in the late 1850s and early 1860s, in *The Geographical Distribution of Animals* (1876), and in *Island Life* (1880) incorporated the manifold data of animal distribution into a unified theory that explained both the existing and past zoological features of the various continents and islands on the basis of geological history and the dispersal and evolution of animals. Wallace's particular synthesis of zoology, geology, and evolution by natural selection, moreover, established a causal framework for zoogeography which dominated that science for nearly a century.

I Toward an Evolutionary Biogeography

One of the major goals of nineteenth-century biogeography was the determination of a set, or sets, of regions which accurately characterized the distribution of animals and plants. An early and influential schema—limited to the world's flora—was that proposed by Candolle, whose *Essai élémentaire de géographie botanique* (Strasbourg, 1820) divided the globe into twenty regions each of which possessed a characteristic (or endemic) flora. During the following four decades, the concept of biogeographical regions gained increased acceptance, although the number and boundaries of such regions varied with different authors. In 1858 P. L. Sclater proposed that the earth was divided into six great ornithological regions—Palearctic (Europe, northern Asia to Japan, and Africa north of the Atlas mountains), Ethiopian (Africa south of the Atlas, southern Arabia, and Madagascar), Oriental or Indian (India, southern Asia, and the western half of the Malay Archipelago), Australian (the eastern half of the Malay Archipelago, Australia, and most of the Pacific Islands), Nearctic (Greenland and North America to north Mexico), and Neotropical (southern Mexico, South America, and the West Indies)—each of which was characterized by a distinct set of bird populations.[2] Using the extensive data from his travels in the Malay Archipelago, Wallace—in an essay "On the Zoological Geography of the Malay Archipelago," written in 1859 and published in the *Journal of the Linnean Society of London (Zoology)* the following year—argued that Sclater's assignment of the western half of the Archipelago to the Indian ornithological region and the eastern half to the Australian region was valid in *every* branch of zoology and, by implication, botany.[3] Surprisingly, the striking differences in the fauna between the eastern and western halves of the Archipelago—marsupials, for instance, are confined to the eastern half (ZG, p. 172)—seemed to be precisely demarcated by the Strait of Lombock (between the islands of Bali and Lombock) which, though merely fifteen miles wide, "marks the limits and abruptly separates two of the great Zoological regions of the globe" (ZG, p. 174). Moreover, the lack of any significant ecological differences between the two halves of the Archipelago implied, for Wallace, that the faunal dissimilarities were the result of past geological configurations vastly different from those of the present and consequent separate evolutionary histories for the now proximate regions.

That the earth's surface had undergone significant changes in time was a central tenet of the new geology—enshrined in Lyell's *Principles of Geology* (1830–1833)—and Wallace, as I pointed out in connection with the 1855 essay "On the Law Which Has Regulated the Introduction of New Species," drew freely upon geological speculation in explaining curious distributional phenomena. He suggested that the faunal similarity of the eastern islands of the Malay Archipelago to New Guinea and Australia suggested a former "great Pacific continent" of which the present islands and Australia are the surviving fragments. Analogously, the faunal similarity of the western islands—including Borneo, Java, and Sumatra—to southern Asia argued for a past "extension of Asia as far to the south and east as the Straits of Macassar and Lombock" (ZG, p. 178). In support of this view, Wallace noted that a "vast submarine plain unites together the apparently disjointed parts of the Indian zoological region . . . so completely that an elevation of only 300 feet would nearly double the extent of tropical Asia" (ZG, p. 179). Most significantly, that plain terminates abruptly in the deep sea of the Moluccas and the Strait of Lombock—that is, at the limit of the Indian region. In his 1857 essay on the distribution of animals in the Aru Islands, Wallace had argued that the shallow seas separating the various islands of the eastern half of the Archipelago implied past land connections between them. The two halves of the Archipelago, therefore, despite their present proximity, belonged to "regions more distinct and contrasted than any other of the great zoological divisions of the globe" (ZG, p. 174). South America and Africa, separated by the vast expanse of the Atlantic, seemed to Wallace not as dramatically different as the Indian and Australian regions. Further, the sharp contrasts between the faunas of the latter two—the presence of elephants, monkeys, orangutans, pheasants, and trogons in the Indian as contrasted to the marsupials, parrots, and birds of paradise of the Australian—are "almost unimpaired at the very limits of their respective districts; so that in a few hours we may experience an amount of zoological difference which only weeks or even months of travel will give us in any other part of the world!" (ZG, p. 174). The boundary between the two regions—later known as "Wallace's Line"—was tentatively fixed by Wallace as coinciding with the deep sea separating Borneo and Celebes in the north to the strait between Bali and Lombock in the south.

"On the Zoological Geography of the Malay Archipelago" is a culmination of Wallace's early views on geographical distribution and places him—at this time—clearly within the continental extensionist tradition. The majority of naturalists (Darwin was a conspicuous exception) invoked postulated past land-bridges and continental extensions of greater or lesser extent to account for present similarities of plants and animals in regions now separated by tracts of water. Specifically, those cases in which islands possessed a rich and varied fauna closely allied with that of adjacent islands or continents forced Wallace to the conclusion that a "geologically recent disruption [had] taken place." Conversely, the distinctness of the faunas of regions now separated by seas—no matter how narrow—implied the lack of any land-connection in, at least, the recent geological past. The great depth of the Strait of Lombock argued for its ancient status and rendered it, despite its narrowness, "an impassable barrier against the passage of any considerable number and variety of land animals" (ZG, pp. 182–83).

It was the island of Celebes which provided Wallace with the clearest evidence for "a bold acceptance of vast changes in the surface of the earth." His analysis of its faunal relationships—which he believed to be "the most anomalous yet known, and in fact altogether unique"—emphasized his adherence to the extensionist position (ZG, p. 177). It also signaled his rejection of the rival hypothesis (of Darwin and a few others) according to which the accidental transport of plants and animals by ocean currents, winds, and floating ice—rather than actual land-connections—sufficed to explain the occurrence of similar species or genera in lands not connected at present. Celebes, near Borneo, was notable for the absence of many of the characteristic animals of either the western or eastern halves of the Malay Archipelago, as well as for the presence of many unique species, and even genera, of birds, mammals, and butterflies. Its endemic fauna, having little or no affinity with those of the adjacent islands but showing a marked similarity to certain African species, suggested "that this island of Celebes is more ancient than most of the islands now surrounding it, and obtained some part of its fauna before they came into existence." The African affinities—a case in which allied species or genera are "distributed in *two* distinct areas separated by countries in which they do not exist"—were anomalous with respect to Wallace's 1855 law "that both species and groups inhabit continuous areas" (ZG, pp. 177–78). By positing a former continent, however, covering a portion at least of what is now the Indian Ocean—and of which Celebes and the African island of Mauritius are among the remaining, widely scattered fragments—Wallace provided a route over which the African forms have reached Celebes.

To support his rejection of the hypothesis of accidental transport, Wallace noted that Celebes—close to Borneo and by virtue of water and air currents "more favourably situated than any other island to receive stray passengers from Borneo, whether drifted across the sea or wafted through the air" (ZG, p. 178)— derived at maximum perhaps 20 percent of its birds and mammals from Borneo. In contrast, Java—separated by a wider sea from Borneo and with sea and air currents which rendered accidental communication between the two islands improbable or difficult— had the majority of its species either identical or closely related to those of Borneo. If accidental transport were the major means of animal and plant dispersal, the proportions should have been reversed. Wallace asserted that the similarities of the faunas of Java and Borneo could only have been produced by a former connection between them, a connection not shared by Celebes. The fauna of Ireland—more than 90 percent of whose species are also found in Great Britain—presents an analogous case and argued for "a very recent separation (long since admitted), to account for these zoological phenomena" (ZG, p. 180).

The distributional patterns on Celebes bore directly on the vexing question of the origin of the flora and fauna of oceanic islands, a question of central significance in the development and testing of evolutionary theory. Taking the island of Madeira, at least four times as distant from south Europe or north Africa as Celebes is from Borneo, Wallace asserted that if transmission across water was a major mechanism for dispersal, then "in a given period a hundred cases of transmission would be more likely to occur" in the case of Celebes than one in the case of Madeira. Yet "of the comparatively rich insect-fauna of Madeira, 40 percent are continental species; and of the flowering plants more than 60 percent." The Canary Islands offered a similarly high proportion of continental species, and Wallace concluded, again, that only a former connection to the mainland could explain "such an amount of specific identity (the weight of which will be very much increased if we take into account the representative species)" (ZG pp. 180–81). The Galápagos Islands, in contrast to Madeira or the Canary Islands, had hardly a species identical to those of the nearest portions of the South American mainland. Wallace argued that these islands probably originated in mid-ocean and thus represented precisely that type of faunal region one would expect to "arise from the chance introduction of a very few species at distant intervals; it is very poor; it contains but few genera, and those scattered among unconnected families; its genera often contain several closely allied species, indicating a single antitype" (ZG, p. 181). Wallace noted that even if the Galápagos had once been united to the mainland, that would have been at so remote a geological epoch "that the natural extinction and renewal of species has left not one in common" between those islands and South America (ZG, p. 181). Thus, the peculiar and apparently endemic fauna of oceanic islands such as the Galápagos or St. Helena, rather than being inexplicable, follows directly from Wallace's assumption that they had no past land-connections and were populated *exclusively* by accidental means of transport, with subsequent evolutionary isolation and divergence.

Wallace concluded his extensionist interpretation of animal distributional data with a reference to Joseph Dalton Hooker's introductory essay to *Flora Novae-Zelandiae* (1853). Hooker had argued that the similarities among the flora of New Zealand, Tasmania, and temperate South America were due to their being remnants of a flora that "had once spread over a larger and more continuous tract of land than now exists in that ocean."[4] Wallace endorsed this hypothesis and declared that the former connection

of New Zealand and other southern islands with the southern
extremity of South America should be of much interest to zoolo-
gists because of

the very satisfactory manner in which this view clears away many
difficulties in the distribution of animals. The most obvious of these is
the occurrence of Marsupials in America only, beyond the Australian
region. They evidently entered by the same route as the plants of
New Zealand and Tasmania which occur in South temperate America
(ZG, p. 183).

That Wallace should explicitly endorse the extensionist position
in a paper which otherwise was a major contribution to the
evolutionist literature—Darwin found the paper *"admirable* in
matter, style and reasoning"—irked Darwin. Acknowledging re-
ceipt of Wallace's Malay paper, which he forwarded to the
Linnean Society for the absent naturalist, Darwin wrote to
Wallace (August 9, 1859) that "I differ *wholly* from you on
colonisation of *oceanic* islands, but you will have *everyone* else
on your side" (ARW, pp. 114–15). Darwin had, in fact, argued
repeatedly with Wallace, Hooker, and others on the problem of
oceanic islands, but had failed to dispel the appeal of the extensionist hypothesis among those whom he regarded as his closest
scientific colleagues.[5] Wallace's Malay essay, therefore, struck
Darwin as problematic because of Wallace's attempt to demonstrate to naturalists that land bridges and other inferences
concerning recent changes in the distribution of land and sea
masses were "among the legitimate deductions of science" (ZG,
p. 181).

The sophisticated association of geographical distribution with
geological changes marks Wallace's 1860 essay as a seminal work
in the evolutionist tradition. He regarded it as laying the theoretical foundation for all his later work in zoogeography, and in
many respects it did. The one aspect of that essay, however, which
is conspicuous by its absence from the developed theory is the
utilization of major continental extensions to explain anomalies
in present distributions. The conversion of Wallace to a position
which made him, finally, a most forceful opponent of the extensionist tradition and the preeminent defender of the doctrine of the
permanence of the continents and oceans was a crucial develop-

ment in nineteenth-century evolutionary science. And while Wallace at this time did not explicitly offer the reasons for his shift—they are made fully clear only later in *The Geographical Distribution of Animals* (1876)—it seems certain that his analysis of global distribution data convinced him that Sclater's sexpartite system had theoretical significance in addition to its obvious descriptive importance. The assumption of the general permanence of the earth's topography—and its corollary of distinct and geologically enduring continents—provided Wallace, as it were, with a *vera causa* for the existence of Sclater's well-defined zoogeographic regions. He was to devote a great portion of his subsequent scientific work and polemicization to the establishment of the thesis that the present distribution of the earth's biota reflected migration and dispersal over a relatively fixed surface, rather than any major alteration or movement of that surface itself in time.

Wallace's essay "On the Physical Geography of the Malay Archipelago" (1863) signals the first major departure from his previous position with respect to the question of continental extensions. He now stressed that land connections could be inferred only in special instances where the geological evidence, as well as distributional data, was overwhelming. Speaking of the intimate connection between the faunal relations of the various islands in the Archipelago (and the Asian and Australian continents), Wallace reiterated his belief that "where we have independent geological evidence, we find that those islands, the productions of which are identical with those of the adjacent countries, have been joined to them within a comparatively recent period, such recent unity being in most cases indicated by the very shallow sea still dividing them."[6] But former land-connections between widely separated regions, as well as between adjacent lands separated by deep seas, were now considered unlikely. Since Wallace held the six zoogeographical regions to represent fundamental divisions in the organic productions of the globe, any connections between them in recent geological epochs became inadmissable. He therefore rejected a land-connection between Celebes—whose anomalous faunal affinities would continue to render its zoogeographical position problematic—and a hypothetical former continent spanning the Indian Ocean to Africa.[7]

Henceforth, Wallace would restrict explanations of distributional patterns to the hypothesis of past migrations across land and sea masses similar in their general outlines to the present oceans and continents.[8]

The 1863 essay elicited the approval of both Lyell and Darwin (to whom it seemed "an epitome of the whole theory of geographical distribution").[9] That it should strike both men as significant is understandable, for Wallace was for the first time fully embracing the theory of the general permanence of the oceans and continents that underlay Lyell's geological uniformitarianism. Wallace's stand was made explicit the following year in his study "On Some Anomalies in Zoological and Botanical Geography." In this paper, he dealt with a number of the issues raised by Darwin in Chapters XI and XII of the *Origin of Species*. As Wallace now endorsed Darwin's general approach to biogeography, he asserted that as "an explanation of the main facts and of many of the special difficulties of geographical distribution, those chapters are in every respect satisfactory."[10] Wallace was, however, less than candid in his assessment. Darwin's treatment of oceanic islands, accidental versus land transport, and the interplay between climatal and geological change (particularly during the Glacial Period) in bringing about the present distribution of animals and plants was far from being in "every respect satisfactory." Darwin's extensive correspondence on these issues and the numerous alterations those two chapters were to undergo in subsequent editions of the *Origin* testify to certain continuing uncertainties.[11] Wallace's own essay treated several cases of apparently anomalous character— "discrepancies which so frequently occur between the distribution of one class or order and another" (SA, p. 111)—which had been advanced as objections to his extension of Sclater's sexpartite system. In so doing, Wallace developed his argument that the six regions represented not merely the most accurate representation of the main facts of ornithological distribution, but also "a true Zoological and Botanical division of the earth" (SA, p. 113). Unlike the various schemes proposed by naturalists which were generally intended to apply only to a particular group of organisms, Wallace claimed that Sclater's divisions were "well adapted to become the foundation for a general system of Ontological regions" (SA, p. 112).

Wallace sought, first, to indicate "how Zoological and Botanical regions are formed, or why organic existences come to be grouped geographically at all" (SA, p. 114). He advanced five premises which he claimed must underlie any discussion of geographical distribution. First, all species have a tendency "to diffuse themselves over a wide area, some one or more in each group being actually found to have so spread" and become —in Darwin's term—"dominant species." Second, there exist "barriers, checking, or absolutely forbidding that diffusion." Third, there has been a continual and "progressive change or replacement of species, by allied forms," throughout the earth's history. Fourth, there has been, *pari passu*, a gradual change in certain features of the earth's surface which has "led to the destruction of old and the formation of new barriers." And last, natural selection entails that these changes of climate and physical conditions will often "favour the diffusion and increase of one group, and lead to the extinction or decrease of another" (SA, p. 114). Given this explanation of the formation of the earth's zoogeographical regions, Wallace then indicated how cases of anomalous distribution could be resolved within the framework of his theoretical model.

Land connections of limited extent still provided the key to certain anomalies. Thus, it had been objected that Japan, which Wallace placed in the Palaearctic Region, should—judging from its snakes—be placed in the Oriental Region. Wallace ingeniously used this very objection to sustain his thesis:

Dr. Gunther informs us ... that snakes are a pre-eminently tropical group, decreasing rapidly in the temperate regions, and absolutely ceasing at 62° N Lat. ... [This fact furnishes] a clue to the peculiarities of the Japanese reptile fauna. For let us suppose that Japan once formed a part of northern Asia (with which it is even now almost connected by two chains of islands), it would then have received its birds, mammals, and batrachians from the Palaearctic region, but there could have been few or no snakes, owing to the much lower curve of the isothermal lines in E. Asia than in W. Europe, giving to Mantchouria a climate as rigorous as that of Sweden.

If at a subsequent period Japan had, through its southern islands, been connected with southern Asia, Wallace argued it could then have acquired a population of Oriental (Indian) snakes, "which would easily establish themselves in an unoccupied region,—whereas the batrachians, as well as the birds and mammals of S. Asia, would find a firmly established Palaearctic population ready to resist the invasion of intruders. . . . It would thus appear that the tropical character of the snakes is quite exceptional, depending upon the fact of the whole group being pre-eminently tropical, and can therefore not be held to throw any doubt on the position of Japan in the Palaearctic zoological region" (SA, pp. 114–15).

Wallace's friend Bates provided him with a more serious test for the hypothesis that the world's zoological and botanical regions coincided with the present distribution of the great land and ocean masses. Bates had shown that portions of the insect fauna of Chile and much of temperate South America showed little connection with that of tropical America, whereas on Wallace's schema there should have been one Neotropical fauna including all of South America, Mexico, and the West Indies. More disturbing were the marked insect affinities between South America and the Australian Region, especially Tasmania and New Zealand (a resemblance which Hooker had shown to characterize also the distribution of plants). Wallace once again generalized from his studies in the Malay Archipelago. There, although there are two distinct zoological regions, certain areas show a mixture of species from the Indo-Malay and Austro-Malay subregions. And in some cases—such as the predominance of certain genera of Oriental (Indian), rather than Australian, insects in New Guinea and the Moluccas (Spice Islands)—the original population had been overwhelmed or, in the extreme, exterminated by immigrants from the adjacent region:

The result is a mixture of races in which the foreign element is in excess; but naturalists need not be bound by the same rule as politicians, and may be permitted to recognise the just claims of the more ancient inhabitants, and to raise up fallen nationalities. The aborigines and not the invaders must be looked upon as the rightful owners of the soil, and should determine the position of their country in our system of Zoological geography. (SA, pp. 118–19)

Because the greater part of southern (temperate) South America was known to be of a more recent date geologically than the tropical mass, it would first have been subject to immigration from the tropics. This would account for the fact that the birds, mammals, and reptiles of temperate South America are modifications of indigenous Neotropical species. Insects and plants, on the other hand, having greater powers of dispersal by "what may be called the adventitious aid of the glacial period and of floating ice" (SA, p. 122) as well as by transoceanic migration, could more easily have travelled the greater distances from the temperate regions of North America or from Australia and Antarctic lands. Being already suited to a temperate climate, these latter would have been capable of establishing themselves successfully in competition with immigrants from the tropical region. The Neotropical Region thus retains its fundamental biogeographical status despite the instances of marked plant and insect affinities with more distant temperate regions.

There remained one remarkable anomaly, the Australian affinities of the marsupial opossums in South America. By 1864, Wallace no longer accepted Hooker's hypothesis of a major southern land connection, which he had supported enthusiastically in the 1860 Malay essay. It now appeared "very doubtful whether these [marsupials] could have been introduced in the same manner as the plants and insects already alluded to, because the latter have to a considerable extent an antarctic character, and do not appear in such numbers as to indicate an actual continuity of land, which would have been almost indispensable for the passage of mammalia, and would at the same time have undoubtedly admitted Australian forms of land birds, which do not exist in South America." Wallace proposed an alternative hypothesis: "It seems more reasonable, therefore, to suppose that these Marsupials have inhabited America since the Eocene period, when the same genus existed in Europe, and the Marsupial order had probably a universal distribution" (SA, pp. 120–21). This is the first public statement of the theory which was to emerge as a keynote of Wallace's zoogeography, namely, the northern origin of organic forms with subsequent migration southward. Certain forms might then become extinct in the more competitive areas of the north and remain as relics in southern regions, protected from evolutionary competition because of the isolation of Australia, temperate South America, and other areas remote from the great continental land masses of the northern hemisphere.

Implicit in these arguments is the doctrine of the general permanence of the great features of the globe. Lyell recognized this when he cited Wallace's solution of the problem of marsupial affinities between Australia and South America, regions which on geological grounds he maintained could not have had a free land connection since the Pliocene or even Miocene epochs.[12] For those anomalous cases which had seemed to require past land connections, Wallace now offered a new framework for investigation:

Though the details of the distribution of the different groups may differ, there will always be more or less general agreement in this respect, because the great physical features of the earth—those which have longest maintained themselves unchanged—wide oceans, lofty mountains, extensive deserts—will have forbidden the intermingling or migration of all groups alike, during long periods of time. The great primary divisions of the Earth for purposes of Natural History, should, therefore, correspond with the great permanent features of the earth's surface—those that have undergone least change in recent geological periods. (SA, p. 122)

Wallace's conviction that the science of zoogeography was predicated upon—indeed rendered intelligible by—the distinct character of the six regions necessitated, almost axiomatically, that the oceans and continents had occupied their present positions at least within the period of development of present species. And while fully aware of the difficulties, conceptual as well as practical, attendant upon any attempt to establish a system of biogeographical regions which would be valid for *all* animals and plants (SA, pp. 122–23), he was to become more insistent that his expanded version of Sclater's system afforded the prime—and most natural—tool for the study of organic distribution. The doctrine of the general permanence of the earth's features assumed a new significance within Wallace's theory, and he would devote a great portion of his scientific work to establish biogeography on the basis of an updated geological uniformitarianism wedded to natural selection.

II *Geographical Distribution of Animals*

Although Wallace had become convinced by 1864 that major past continental extensions were inadmissible, the predominant scientific opinion still held to some form of the extensionist hypothesis. Hooker's 1866 address on "Insular Floras," delivered before the British Association for the Advancement of Science at Nottingham, testifies to the then perplexed state of distribution theory.[13] Primarily a description of the floras of oceanic islands and their relation to those of continents, Hooker's address included a pointed analysis of the two rival explanations for the stocking of oceanic islands with plants from a continent: "either seeds were carried across the ocean by currents, or the winds, or birds, or similar agencies; or the islands once formed part of the continent, and the plants spread over intermediate land that has since disappeared."[14] Hooker, though now inclining to the hypothesis of transoceanic dispersal, made it clear that it was not then possible to arrive at a scientific verdict because the difficulties facing each hypothesis were great. Moreover, as he wrote to Darwin, he would now have to "meet a host who are all on the continental side—in fact, pretty nearly all the thinkers."[15]

The appearance of Andrew Murray's *Geographical Distribution of Mammals* in 1866 heightened the sense of inadequacy in the scientific treatment of the entire subject of distribution. Wallace wrote Darwin that he found Murray to possess "some good ideas here and there, but [he] is quite unable to understand Natural Selection, and makes a most absurd mess of his criticism of your views on oceanic islands." Wallace then suggested that a volume by Darwin on distribution would be most interesting (ARW, p. 149). Darwin replied—in characteristic tone—that he doubted "whether I shall ever have strength" to treat the matter in any fuller detail than in the *Origin* (ARW, p. 150), adding (to

Hooker) that he did not "suppose any man could master so comprehensive a subject as it has now become, if all kingdoms of nature are included. I have read Murray's book, and am disappointed."[16] That Murray was an extensionist, in addition to being incapable of mastering the intricacies of natural selection, made the absence of a treatise which resolved the problems of distribution successfully—and within the evolutionist/dispersal framework—more critical. Wallace again wrote to Darwin, in 1868, of the importance of a work on distribution and noted, as an afterthought, that he found Lyell's chapter on oceanic islands in the second volume of the tenth edition of the *Principles of Geology* (1868) very good. Darwin also was much pleased with Lyell's chapter, which was one of the major additions to the new edition of the *Principles* (ARW, pp. 173–74).

The chapter on oceanic islands was, however, not the only subject to attract Wallace and Darwin to Lyell's revised edition. In addition to Lyell's famed, if (ultimately) ambiguous, public endorsement of the theory of evolution by natural selection, there appeared in the first volume a considerably augmented account of recent geological theories. Preeminent among these were hypotheses concerning the various causes of the glacial epoch and the compelling evidence for, and detailed description of, Pleistocene glaciation. The decade of the 1860s had been one of intense interest in glacial phenomena and the concept of the "Ice Age." Wallace followed the geologists' controversies on the possible causes of glaciation closely and was at the center of several of them. The concept of a "recent Ice Age" had been brought to the attention of British scientists by the early 1840s, notably through the efforts of the Swiss naturalist Louis Agassiz. But it was not until the 1860s that Pleistocene glaciation became established as a working hypothesis in Great Britain.[17] Wallace was alert to the implications of glacial theory for his own work: he now could invoke the glacial epoch as among "the most powerful agents in causing the dispersal of all kinds of organisms, and thus bringing about the actual distribution that now prevails" (ML, II, 100), without the necessity of positing vast former continental changes.

By 1868–1869, then, Wallace had at hand all the elements for a comprehensive treatment of zoogeography: glaciation, the permanence of the oceans and continents (with auxiliary minor changes in physical geography), methods of dispersal and migration of organisms, and, of course, evolution by natural selection. He was thus prepared to accede to the request of Darwin and "Professor A. Newton and Dr. Sclater, who urged me to undertake a general review of the geographical distribution of animals" (ML, II, 94). The resulting treatise—*The Geographical Distribution of Animals*—appeared in 1876 and was recognized at once as a landmark in the science of zoogeography as well as a strategic contribution to evolutionary theory.[18]

Geographical Distribution is comprised of four parts dealing, respectively, with the principles and general phenomena of animal distribution, the geographical distribution of extinct animals, the faunal and environmental characteristics of the six zoogeographical regions and their major subregions (zoological geography), and the actual range of the main families and genera of land animals (geographical zoology). Species, as such, were disregarded because Wallace considered them too numerous to provide the basis for any manageable distributional analysis. Moreover, because they represent the most recent evolutionary modifications, he deemed them less indicative than genera—"the natural groups of species"—of those fundamental distributional patterns connected with the more permanent features of the earth's history.[19] Wallace decided to omit man from this study of the animal kingdom because to treat the genus *Homo* zoogeographically would yield the uninformative statement "universally distributed." To deal, on the other hand, with the distribution of the "varieties" or "races" of man would have violated the major methodological premise of the work. For Wallace, anthropology had now become "a science by itself [which] it seems better to omit . . . altogether from a zoological work, than to treat it in a necessarily superficial manner" (GD, I, viii–ix).

Wallace intended this treatise—as he did nearly all his writings—for the nonscientific reader as well as the professional scientist, that is, for anyone "capable of understanding Lyell's 'Principles,' or Darwin's 'Origin '" (GD, I, xii). *Geographical Distribution* is an excellent specimen of Victorian science writing that is at once lucid and rigorous. The interweaving of fact, theory, and descriptive prose—which Wallace had practiced in *A Narrative of Travels on the Amazon and Rio Negro* and perfected in *The Malay Archipelago*—is masterful and ranks with that of the *Origin* itself. Particularly notable is the series of plates Wallace had executed to illustrate the physical aspect and characteristic fauna of the more important zoogeographical subregions, so as to "make the book more intelligible to those readers who have no special knowledge of systematic zoology, and to whom most of the names with which its pages are often crowded must necessarily be unmeaning" (GD, I, x).

Part One, "The Principles and General Phenomena of Distribution," summarizes the theories Wallace had been developing since the late 1850s and extends his analysis of the Malay Archipelago to include all of the world's chief zoogeographical regions. To explain why different regions possess distinct and characteristic fauna—why, for example, parts of South Africa have lions, antelopes, zebras, and giraffes, while climatically similar parts of Australia house only kangaroos, wombats, phalangers, and mice—Wallace invokes evolutionary change in conjunction with geographic "isolation by the most effectual and most permanent barriers" (GD, I, 7–8). Wallace emphasized that the different classes of animals are (and were) not equally effective in overcoming the obstacles which tend to limit their natural tendency to increase their range. Thus, some physical obstacles are easily overcome by certain mammals whose powers of dispersal make their potential range virtually unlimited. The elephant, for example, climbs mountains, "traverses rivers with great ease and forces its way through the densest jungle" (GD, I, 11). Other animals—such as the apes and lemurs who, restricted to an aboreal life, can never roam far beyond the limits of forest vegetation—are confined to specific habitats and find mountains, rivers, or deserts absolutely impassable. Climate also limits the range of certain groups of animals. Finally, the seas are perhaps the most effective barriers to the dispersal of animals, with very few mammals, in particular, capable of swimming over any considerable extent of water (GD, I, 11–14).

Wallace placed great stress—as did Edward Forbes and Darwin, among others—upon the effects of glaciation in bringing about present global distribution patterns (ARW, p. 203). As the climate of the northern hemisphere became colder, he argued, animals and plants would have been pushed southwards before the advancing glaciers, populating the (now) temperate regions with arctic forms. Wallace considered botanical data to be one of the strongest confirmations of the existence of a past ice age. As the earth's climate cooled, northern plants would have migrated to lowlands in the more temperate regions. When the climate improved and the glaciers retreated north, these plants would then "necessarily travel in two directions, back towards the arctic circle and up towards the alpine peaks." Contemporary mountain flora should—on this hypothesis—be related more to arctic forms than to the flora of surrounding plains, and Wallace noted that the plants of the Pyrenees are typically Scandinavian. In "the celebrated case of the White Mountains in New Hampshire ... all the plants on the summit are arctic species, none of which exist in the lowlands for near a thousand miles further north" (GD, I, 42–43). Conversely, in those cases where glaciation cannot have so acted, mountain vegetation would not possess an arctic character. Wallace cited as a striking confirmation of the glacial thesis the fact that the flora of the mountain peaks of Teneriffe (in the Canary Islands) is not related to northern plants—arctic species having been prevented from reaching those oceanic islands beyond the reach of the glaciers—but to those of the surrounding lower elevations.

Mammals provided Wallace with much of the data he used to sustain his zoogeographical hypotheses. Not only were they the best-studied animals at that time (and hence those whose actual ranges were known most accurately), but they were especially suitable for the reconstruction of past distributional patterns. Because their dispersal is (generally) dependent upon the configuration of land masses, they afford more direct evidence of the past condition of the earth's surface than other classes of animals—insects, for example—which are greatly subject to dispersal by agencies such as wind or water currents. These latter "tend to obliterate the effect of natural barriers, and produce a scattered distribution," the origins of which must necessarily remain obscure (GD, I, 57). Also, mammalian fossil remains were among the most extensively known in 1876 and provided one of the surest guides for the relatively young sciences of paleozoology and paleogeography.

Paleontological data were crucial in the development of evolutionary theory, and Wallace devoted the second part of *Geographical Distribution* to a detailed analysis of the distribution of extinct mammals, with brief comments on extinct birds, reptiles, insects, and land and fresh-water mollusks. Though the significance of fossils for theoretical biogeography was generally recognized in 1876, Wallace related their geographical and geological distribution to modern animal distribution in an original and forceful manner. He sought to "determine what portion of the existing races of animals in a country are descendants of its ancient fauna, and which are comparatively modern immigrants" (GD, I, 107). Because the distribution of animals found fossil is not identical with the distribution of living forms allied to them, Wallace argued that it was possible to reconstruct past migration routes in order to locate the probable origin of existing genera and families. He emphasized that his "great object [was] to trace back, step by step, the varying distribution of the chief forms of life; and to deduce, wherever possible, the physical changes which must have accompanied or caused such changes" (GD, I, 108).

The third and fourth parts of *Geographical Distribution*—dealing with the faunal characteristics of the zoogeographical regions and with the present range of each of the families and genera of vertebrates, insects, and mollusks—constitute the core of Wallace's argument. There, a vast array of data drawn from the past and present distributions of animals is deployed to sustain the thesis that all the chief types of animal life appear to have originated in the great northern continents and then migrated southwards into the unoccupied continents of the Southern Hemisphere. These latter—now represented by South America, Australia, and South Africa (with Madagascar)—have been "more or less completely isolated, during long periods, both from the northern [land masses] and from each other," but have been subject to immigration of northern animals during those rare periods when they had more closely approached, or actually were connected to, the northern continents (GD, I, 173–74).

Wallace's synthesis of geological and zoological data is complex but may be outlined as follows. The great land masses of the north are of immense antiquity and comprise the area in which the earliest vertebrates and (probably) insects and land-mollusks originated. The status of the Nearctic and Palaearctic regions was a controversial issue, but Wallace considered that whatever their past land connections, the two regions ranked as distinct and fundamental ones. He maintained that during the Eocene and Miocene periods, the distinction between them was, in fact, greater than at present. Owing to a deterioration of climate, the Nearctic region "suffered a considerable diminution of [its] productive area, and has in consequence lost a number of its more remarkable forms." The dissimilarity between the two northern temperate regions appears, therefore, less striking than it actually is. At an early period, the Oriental and Palaearctic regions probably shared a similar climate and fauna, but the elevation of the Himalayan mountains (which Wallace placed after the Miocene) caused an abrupt and permanent physical and climatic barrier. Many of the animals which—according to the fossil evidence—once were common to both regions would then have become restricted to either the northern or southern side of the Himalayan chain. Thereafter, the Palaearctic developed its characteristic fauna and the Oriental its typical tropical forms (GD, II, 154–60).

The southern continents, according to Wallace, had been colonized from the north, but at different times and along different routes. Australia appeared to have had but one such union—with the Palaearctic land mass at a remote era—by means of which it received the ancestors of its marsupials and monotremata (GD, II, 155). Its long subsequent isolation from any other continent accounts for the evolution of its unique fauna, which exhibits the "development of a primeval type of mammal, almost wholly uninfluenced by any incursions of a later and higher type" (GD, II, 161). The evolutionary histories of the Neotropical and Ethiopian regions were more complicated. Each appeared, to Wallace, to have had several successive unions with northern continents—the Neotropical with North America and the Ethiopian with Eurasia. South America first received—during the late Mesozoic—the ancestors of its edentates and rodents, when these were among the highest mammals then evolved. Subsequent isolation allowed for a rich development and diversification of these early mammals before the Neotropical was again united to the Nearctic region in the early Cenozoic. It would have then received the ancestors of its marmosets, monkeys, and early carnivores. Later still, another Nearctic connection would have brought its llamas, peccaries, deer, tapirs, and opossums (GD, II, 81–82). These successive waves of increasingly highly evolved animals from the north—which in some cases supplanted more primitive forms and in others continued to coexist with lower types—account, according to Wallace's theory, for the rich and varied present-day fauna of the Neotropical Region (GD, II, 80–83). Southern Africa, like South America, had been connected to northern land masses at several periods—but to the Palaearctic and Oriental Regions rather than to the Nearctic—with the result that the Ethiopian Region also reflects an intermingling of distinct and successive faunas. The earlier immigrants are represented by the lemurs and insectivora, while the latter immigrants include the antelope, the giraffe, the elephant, the rhinoceros, and the lion (GD, I, 285–92). Wallace emphasized that each of the southern continents derived its fauna "independently, and perhaps at very different times, from the north, with which they therefore have a true genetic relation" (GD, II, 159). The affinities between parts of the fauna (and flora) of Australia, South America, and South Africa—which were held by some naturalists to imply a former southern land-connection—he deemed superficial, indicating either isolated remnants of widespread northern immigration or incidences of accidental transport (GD, I, 174).

Because anomalous distributions posed a fundamental problem for nineteenth-century biogeographers, Wallace regarded his particular resolution of those anomalies as crucial to the success of his theories. The tapirs, for example, are represented today by species inhabiting South America and parts of Malaysia, but no intervening regions. Fossil remains, however, indicated that ancestral tapirs existed in India (in the Miocene), in North America (in the Miocene), and in Europe (as early as the lower Eocene). Wallace concluded that the tapirs were once a widespread group which had become extinct, by the late Pliocene, in the Palaearctic and Nearctic regions, leaving modern descendants only in the extremes of its former range (GD, I, 122 and II, 212–13). The family *Camelidae* was another example of a once widespread group whose modern representatives—camels in the Palaearctic and llamas and alpacas in South America—inhabit discontinuous regions. Wallace invoked the case as "a warning against the too common practice of assuming the direct land connection of remote continents, in order to explain similar instances of discontinuous distribution to that of the present family" (GD, II, 216–17). The order Marsupialia—confined now to Australia and South and North America (the true opossums)—posed a more troublesome anomaly. Wallace maintained, as he had in the 1864 essay on distribution, that fossil marsupials dating from the late Eocene in Europe were the ancestors of the South American opossums (GD, II, 249). But because no definite early marsupial fossils had been discovered in the Oriental region—from which they would necessarily have had to come to colonize Australia on Wallace's hypothesis—his assertion that the marsupials' present discontinuous distribution derives from their being remnants of a once widespread northern group remained merely a supposition.[20]

The *Geographical Distribution of Animals* is the culmination of Wallace's efforts to forge a rigorous and coherent science of zoogeography. Commited to the doctrine of the general permanence of the oceans and continents—he declared that since at least "the dawn of the Tertiary period we still find our six regions, or what may be termed the rudiments of them, already established" (GD, II, 159)—Wallace demonstrated how the known agents of animal dispersion were sufficient to determine the probable birthplace and subsequent geographical history of the more important genera and families without positing vast major changes in physical geography. Darwin considered the book a "grand and memorable work, which will last for years as the foundation for all future treatises" on zoogeography (ARW, p. 235). Darwin's prediction was an accurate one and serves as a fitting assessment of the significance of Wallace's achievement. Certain qualifications, however, are in order.

Though Wallace had laid down the guidelines which were to govern zoogeographical research and theory formulation for nearly a century, many details of his broad synthesis have been sucessfully challenged. The boundaries between the major zoo-geographical regions and subregions have necessarily been re-vised as more accurate and extensive distributional data have been forthcoming, and the methods of analyzing those data made more sophisticated. The border between the Oriental and Austra-lian Regions—to cite the most famous example—has been shifted repeatedly by zoogeographers and is no longer considered to be defined by "Wallace's Line."[21] Wallace himself had offered his boundary as provisional, noting that the precise limits between regions—when not formed by oceans—were somewhat arbitrary and "will be, not a defined line but a neutral territory of greater or less width, within which the forms of both regions will inter-mingle" (GD, I, 184). Similarly, increased fossil evidence has required modifications in Wallace's reconstruction of past con-tinental configurations (and connections) and the former distri-bution and migrations of animals. The thesis of the northern origin of the major orders and families of mammals has been effectively criticized. The higher primates—the Old World mon-keys, apes, and the ancestors of man—for example, are now thought to have emerged most probably in Africa and thence spread across the globe.[22] Most significantly, the recent compelling evidence for continental drift has provided a radical alternative to Wallace's explanation for the similarities between the fauna (and flora) of the southern continents. Given these qualifications, it remains true that the general principles advanced in *Geogra-phical Distribution* were fundamental to the development of the science of zoogeography. And Wallace's position as the leading student of animal distribution was confirmed, four years later, with the appearance of *Island Life*.

III   Island Life (1880)

The fauna and flora of islands had intrigued, and often puzzled, naturalists at least since the appearance of J. R. Forster's *Observations Made During a Voyage Round the World* (1778). Data from the Galápagos Islands, to cite the most famous example, were prominent in both Darwin's and Wallace's initial formulations of evolutionary theory; those drawn from the Malay

Archipelago were fundamental to the latter's zoogeographical theories. *Island Life*—which Darwin considered the best book Wallace had published and which Hooker thought "an immense advance [which] . . . brushed away more cobwebs that have obscured the subject than any other" treatise (ARW, pp. 252, 289–90)—is an analysis of the distributional phenomena presented by islands in their complex relation to each other and to continents. Although much of the first part of the book—dealing with the mode of variation, modification, and dispersal of organisms and with past geological and climatal changes—follows directly from *Geographical Distribution of Animals*, *Island Life* is an original and major extension of Wallace's biogeographical system. The plan of the 1876 work had required that he treat mainly genera and the higher orders of animals. *Island Life*, in contrast, focuses on species and includes important discussions of phytogeography (plant distribution), thus providing a more comprehensive scope for Wallace's theorization.

Because many islands, on Wallace's (and Darwin's) hypothesis, can *not* originally have been colonized by animals and plants migrating across land bridges, he devoted a chapter to the facilities for transmission over water of various organisms. Land mammals, for example, are effectively barred from traveling across expanses of sea, and even those that swim well—pigs and deer—would, he argued, never venture far from coastal regions. They would, therefore, not be expected to constitute part of the fauna of true oceanic islands. Smaller (especially arboreal) mammals, however, can be transported on floating trees or "rafts" (masses of soil with trees and shrubs growing on them) and thus occasionally be carried great distances across the sea.[23] Birds are capable of sustained flight and can cross water barriers more effectively than can mammals. Smaller birds, Wallace noted, may involuntarily be carried great distances— such as from Europe to the Azores—by violent gales. Land reptiles, like small mammals, might also be transported on floating trees and thus colonize islands. The eggs (and even small adult forms) of amphibia and fresh-water fish, Wallace suggested, might be carried from lakes and rivers to islands by hurricanes or waterspouts. Moreover, because these eggs are capable of being frozen without injury, they can be carried in floating ice. Wallace considered that the widespread distribution of newts and salamanders, for example, in the Northern Hemisphere may have resulted from such a mode of dispersal. Insects, of all land animals, have the most extensive means of dispersal over water. Not only do they possess great powers of flight, but because of their extreme lightness they can be carried great distances by winds. Moreover, insects can often survive in sea water for many days and be carried long distances safely by ocean currents. Wallace suggested, too, that insects eggs and larvae often inhabit solid timber and could be carried on floating trees. Land and fresh-water mollusks—the last groups of animals discussed—were quite limited in their means of dispersal in sea water, but Wallace considered that they, also, could probably survive occasional transport. The eggs of fresh-water mollusks were known to become attached to the feet of aquatic birds and would thus be capable of wide diffusion over water (IL, pp. 75–79).

Wallace next discussed plant dispersal, noting that plants have far greater possibilities for migration than animals. Their seeds or spores are extremely hardy and can lie dormant for many years and then vegetate, enduring extremes of heat, of cold, of drought, or of moisture which would be fatal to animal eggs. Since plant seeds are also generally light and often have winged or hooked appendages, it is clear that they are susceptible of being carried great distances by ocean currents, rivers, winds, icebergs, and by birds and other animals (IL, pp. 80–81).

Since some islands have not always existed as such—having had one or more land connections (or closer approach) to continents in former ages—migration over land would also have contributed to the distributional patterns of certain present-day insular faunas and floras. In addition to a résumé of those past geographical and geological changes he had discussed fully in *Geographical Distribution*, Wallace considered in some detail the influence of past climatal alterations on the dispersal of animals and plants. Of these, Wallace maintained (as he had suggested in 1876) that glacial epochs and "that still more extraordinary climatic phenomenon—the mild climate and luxuriant vegetation of the Arctic zone" played fundamental roles in bringing about the present distribution of organic forms (IL, pp. 123–24). He devoted three extensive chapters—which he told Darwin constituted the "very foundation-stone of the book" (ARW, p. 251) —to the controversial question of the causes, extent, and consequences of glacial epochs and intervening warm periods.

Wallace, as I noted before, early recognized the biogeographical significance of glaciation. He now presented a cogent review of the evidence that had been accumulated to "prove the recent occurrence of glacial epochs in the temperate regions" of the Northern Hemisphere (IL, p. 107). The marks left by the advance and retreat of glaciers—rounded or smoothed rocks occurring over whole valleys and mountain sides (*roches moutonnées*), for example—he regarded as indisputable testimony to the fact that large land masses in Europe and North America had once been covered by vast sheets of ice. The profound effect this great climatal cycle had upon the distribution of all living things was clear:

When an icy mantle crept gradually over much of the northern hemisphere till large portions of Europe and North America were reduced to the condition of Greenland now, the greater part of the animal life must have been driven southward, causing a struggle for existence, which must have led to the extermination of many forms, and the migration of others into new areas. But these effects must have been greatly multiplied and intensified if, as there is very good reason to believe, the glacial epoch itself—or at least the earlier and later phases of it—consisted of two or more alternations of warm and cold periods. (IL, p. 117)

Evidence that the climates of Pleistocene interglacial periods were, in fact, warmer than climates at present was abundant. Wallace cited the fossil remains of the hippopotamus in England and of the elephant and rhinoceros in Switzerland—animals whose present distribution is entirely tropical—as proof that the glacial periods had been instrumental in bringing about the striking differences in northern and southern fauna (and flora) that now prevail. Many northern species would have become extinct or gradually been driven far southwards, where their modern descendants now live, while other species would have gradually become modified in response to colder climatal conditions to produce contemporary arctic and temperate forms (IL, pp. 119–23).

While the existence of past widespread glaciation was generally accepted by 1880, there was an intense dispute in the scientific community as to the actual cause (or causes) of glacial epochs. Some held that the original heat of the earth had decreased, or that the amount of heat radiated by the sun or the temperature of space had varied, thus bringing the onset of glaciation. Others maintained that astronomical factors—such as variations in the tilt of the earth's axis or variations in the eccentricity (shape) of the earth's elliptical orbit combined with the effects of the precession of the equinoxes—caused fluctuations in the amount of solar energy received by the earth extreme enough to produce glacial conditions. Finally, others—notably Lyell—argued that changes in the distribution and elevation of the earth's sea and land masses had caused those extreme alterations in climate which the geological record shows to have occurred (IL, pp. 125–26). Of these varied hypotheses, Wallace concluded that it had been an appropriate juxtaposition of astronomical and geographical influences which rendered conditions possible for the onset (and retreat) of glaciation.

In propounding a novel solution—he told Darwin that he believed he had "found the true explanation of geological climates" (ARW, p. 251)—Wallace combined elements of Lyell's hypothesis with the views of James Croll, whose *Climate and Time* (1875) was the most forceful advocacy of astronomical causes as the agents of glaciation. Wallace held that although favorable conditions brought about as a consequence of the earth's motion (such as when periods of high orbital eccentricity effected severe winter climates) were prerequisites for a glacial epoch, they were not by themselves sufficient. Only when the great northern land masses had become consolidated (as they did during parts of the Pleistocene)—effectively shutting out the northerly flow of warmer currents from their interiors and from the arctic region—would a widespread and intense glacial epoch be rendered possible (IL, p. 536). Conversely, the mild arctic climates which characterized much of the Miocene, Eocene, and still earlier Periods—as proved by the abundant fossil remains of now temperate or tropical forms—were, Wallace continued, due to the comparatively fragmentary and insular condition of the great north temperate lands throughout much of the earth's history. Such conditions would have allowed a greater influx of warm currents into the Arctic (IL, pp. 187–89, 190–96, 201–202). Wallace emphasized that his explanation of climatal change obviated the most serious objection to Croll's astronomical argument, namely "its being thought to lead *necessarily* to frequently recurring glacial epochs throughout all geological time" (IL, p. 208). Rather—as the lack of any evidence for frequent glacial epochs demanded—widespread glaciation would not have arisen each time astronomical conditions were suitable, but only when the requisite geographical conditions were also available (IL, pp. 179–81, 208–209). Wallace's attempt to resolve a strictly geological controversy—albeit one which had a great bearing on biological history—is one more example of his wide-ranging and imaginative scientific theorizing. It was regarded at the time as among the more plausible solutions to the complex question of the causes of glacial epochs, a question which geologists have still not answered completely.[24]

Wallace was compelled to deal with one other contentious issue—the sufficiency of geological time for evolution—before he could turn to the central question of the origin of insular faunas and floras. The theory of natural selection, as originally propounded, required an immensely long earth's history to allow for that slow and gradual selection (and accumulation) of random variations which was the mechanism of evolutionary change. Uniformitarian geology, by providing a time-scale of vast magnitude, had been an integral element in securing the initial acceptance of evolutionary biology. For, assuming the correctness of the calculations of Lyell, Darwin, and Huxley, among others, the earliest forms of life must have appeared (Wallace estimated) at the latest 500 million years ago (IL, pp. 211–12). Shortly after the publication of the *Origin of Species*, however, William Thomson (Lord Kelvin) and other physicists argued, from seemingly incontrovertible thermodynamical calculations, that the earth had solidified from its initial molten state between 20 and 400 million years ago.[25] The challenge to the geologists and the evolutionary biologists appeared formidable: their estimates for the existence of life on earth far exceeded the age of the earth itself as permitted by the physicists' calculations. Kelvin, whose scientific authority was impressive, increasingly inclined to the smaller figure of approximately 20 million years and loomed before Darwin as an "odious spectre" (ARW, p. 220). Cognizant of the threat to evolutionary theory, Darwin attempted—unsuccessfully—in later editions of the *Origin* to reconcile the conflicting time-scales.[26] The controversy was still acute in 1880 and Wallace, drawing upon ideas he had adumbrated in an earlier article, proposed his own solution in *Island Life*.[27]

While still upholding the general principles of the uniformitarian geologists, Wallace now endorsed the view that the *rate* of geological change had been faster in the past than it was at present. If the sun had generated more heat formerly—Kelvin and most physicists argued that the sun was a cooling body, dissipating its limited store of energy by radiation[28]—then terrestrial forces such as winds, rains, oceanic currents, volcanic eruptions, and the upheaving of mountains, would have been more violent in the past (IL, pp. 223–24). The frequent recurrence of periods of high and low orbital eccentricity would have accentuated the severity of past climatal alterations (IL, p. 230). Since natural selection operates on variations which tend to render organisms more or less fit for their environments, Wallace reasoned that a more rapid rate of environmental change—a more frequent joining and sundering of adjacent land or more abrupt climatal shifts, for example—would subject "the whole flora and fauna of a country at comparatively short intervals" to an intensified struggle for existence:

Some species would stand the change better than others, while it is highly probable that some would be actually benefited by it, and that others would be injured. But the benefited would certainly increase, and the injured decrease, in consequence, and thus a series of changes would be initiated that might lead to most important results. Again, we are sure that some species would become modified in adaptation to the change of climate more readily than others, and these modified species would therefore increase at the expense of others not so readily modified. (IL, pp. 230–31)

Both the extinction of certain species and the evolution of new varieties, and ultimately of new species, would, then, have been decidedly more rapid in earlier stages of the history of life. Given this more rapid rate of both geological and organic change, Wallace could conclude that the time-scale "thus arrived at is immensely less than the usual estimates of geologists, and is so far within the limits of the duration of the earth as calculated by Sir William Thomson, as to [still] allow for the development of the lower organisms an amount of time anterior to the Cambrian period several times greater than has elapsed between that period and the present day"(IL, p. 236).

To support his contention that evolution by natural selection could be accommodated within the framework of a drastically shortened time-scale, Wallace noted that the period since the close of the last Ice Age had been one of uniform and unusually low orbital eccentricity. During this time—which Wallace considered approximately 60,000 years—mutations of climate would have been relatively unimportant and the earth's temperate zones, in particular, would "have enjoyed *an exceptional stability of climate*." In the absence of those major climatal changes which operate to accelerate the modifications, migrations, and extinctions of species, organic forms would be able to adapt themselves to the slight changes that did occur "without much disturbance." The result, Wallace concluded, "would be *an epoch of exceptional stability of species*" (IL, p. 232). To use this limited—and, in his view, atypical—perspective to establish a scale against which to measure all geological and evolutionary change was misleading and had led the uniformitarians, according to Wallace, into the error of exaggerating geological time. Wallace's attempted resolution of the conflict between evolutionary biology and late nineteenth-century physics —plausible but unsubstantiated—provides a striking example of the vulnerability of the theory of natural selection (as opposed to simply evolution) to a broad spectrum of scientific, as well as philosophical and religious, objections (ARW, pp. 325–26). Ironically, the threat posed by the physicists was later shown to be only apparent. The discovery of radioactivity by Henri Becquerel in 1896, and Pierre Curie's announcement in 1903 that radium salts continually release heat energy, effectively repudiated Kelvin's assumption that there was no source of energy to replace that which the sun lost by radiation.[29] The path was open for new and more reliable methods of calculating the age of the various geological strata and their fossils. As a consequence, the age of the earth is now reckoned at more than 4 billion years, far in excess of that demanded by even the most prodigal uniformitarians.

With the parameters of geochronology and geological climates clarified, Wallace turned, in the second part of *Island Life,* to the specific question of the origin and characteristics of insular floras and faunas. Islands, because of their restricted areas and definite boundaries and their well-defined assemblages of species, offer more precise units for biogeographical analysis than do continental areas. Since "in most cases their geographical and biological limits coincide," islands provide unique opportunities for studying the laws and phenomena of distribution and afforded Wallace "experimental" tests, as it were, for the theories enunciated more generally in 1876 (IL, p. 241).

Islands are classified as either "continental" or "oceanic," depending upon whether they once were parts of continental land masses—"of which they are but detached fragments"—or had originated in mid-ocean. Following Darwin, who had been the first to call attention to their biological significance, Wallace defined oceanic islands as "of volcanic or coralline formation, usually far from continents and always separated from them by very deep sea." As a consequence of their never having had continental connections, oceanic islands contain no indigenous land mammals or amphibians. Moreover, those animals and plants which do (now) inhabit oceanic islands—such as the Galápagos, St. Helena, the Azores, and Bermuda—"must either themselves have reached them by crossing the ocean, or be the descendants of ancestors who did so" (IL, pp. 242–45).

Continental islands, in contrast, are rarely remote from adjacent continents and "always contain some land mammals and amphibia, as well as representatives of the other classes and orders in considerable variety" (IL, p. 243). Wallace further distinguished between "ancient" and "recent" continental islands. The latter—which include Great Britain and Ireland, Borneo,

Java, Japan, and Formosa—possess all the characteristics of a portion of a continent separated from it at a recent geological period. They are situated on submerged banks separated by a shallow sea from the mainland, they resemble the continent in their geological formation, and their animals and plants are identical, or closely allied, to those of the neighboring mainland. Ancient continental islands—typified by Madagascar—differ from those of more recent origin by their being separated from the mainland by an expanse of deep sea. And while they possess land mammals and amphibians, as well as all the other classes of animals and plants, in relative abundance, these are usually highly distinct species forming many peculiar genera or families (IL, p. 244). Finally, there are "anomalous islands"—such as Celebes and New Zealand—which, because they combine the characteristics of both continental and oceanic islands, present unique problems for biogeographical analysis (IL, pp. 541–42).

The Azores, a group of nine widely scattered islands situated to the southwest of Europe—of which the largest, San Miguel, is nearly 900 miles from the coast of Portugal—are typical oceanic islands. Their considerable distance from the nearest continent, the great depth of the intervening sea, and their volcanic structure "render it in the highest degree improbable that the Azores have ever been united with the European continent." As expected, they possess no indigenous land mammals or amphibians, nor any reptiles or freshwater fish, "although the islands are sufficiently extensive, possess a mild and equable climate, and are in every way adapted to support all these groups." Those small mammals, such as rabbits, weasels, rats, and mice, which are now found wild in the Azores, Wallace considered to have been introduced by man. The indigenous animals—those that originally reached the islands by natural means—consisted (except for one species of European bat), therefore, of birds, insects, and land shells (IL, pp. 247–49).

Of the fifty-three species of birds that had been observed at the Azores, the greater proportion (thirty-one) were "either aquatic or waders—birds of great powers of flight, whose presence in the remotest islands is by no means remarkable" (IL, p. 249). Of the resident land-birds, all except one (the Azorean bullfinch) were common in Europe and North Africa, and Wallace maintained that they had all originated as "stragglers," having been blown out to sea by storms and landing on the islands by chance. Frequent storms in the vicinity of the Azores would have continued to bring similar immigrants, thus ensuring a constant supply of continental specimens. Sustained intermingling would prevent the Azorean species from the evolutionary divergence (from parent stocks) that would otherwise be expected on remote islands in the mid-Atlantic possessing environmental conditions far different from those of the mainland. The single endemic bullfinch was, actually, more representative of the bird fauna of oceanic islands. It demonstrated clearly the special modifications that a particular species—given the amount of individual variation always present in any population—could develop under isolated conditions. Wallace suggested that the bullfinch, as a nonmigratory bird inhabiting woody districts, would have been blown to sea only in the rarest and most unlikely instances. The original stock would, thus, not have been subjected to continued interbreeding with new arrivals and would have evolved sufficiently to rank as a non-European species (IL, pp. 251–52). Most other oceanic islands—such as the Galápagos, St. Helena, and the Sandwich Islands—possess far more endemic species and genera of birds than do the Azores and are more indicative of the long-continued specialization and divergence that characterize the organic forms of such islands. As a further explanation of the nearly complete identity of Azorean and European species of birds, Wallace suggested that during the glacial epoch the Azores—whose latitude icebergs reach even now—would have been among those oceanic islands subject to the effects of the glaciation that covered so much of North America and Europe. The climate of these islands would have become sufficiently rigorous to effect the extinction of its more ancient bird fauna. The present Azorean birds would, thus, date from the postglacial period and would not be expected to have diverged in any significant way from continental species in so short a geological time.

Some Azorean insects are also similar, or identical, to common European species, and their presence is explained by the same causes as those which served to introduce birds to the islands. However, among the indigenous beetles—the most numerous insects in the Azores—many species are altogether peculiar to these islands, with two so distinct as to constitute new genera. Wallace held that owing to the greater powers of endurance of insects (or their eggs), a number of species could have survived the glacial epoch and these now represent a portion of a more ancient fauna which had migrated to the islands in preglacial times. The affinities of certain Azorean insect species to those of South America and Madagascar, rather than to Europe, indicated, to Wallace, that they were relicts of an ancient and once widely distributed group now confined to the fringes of its former range. The land-shells of the Azores also present a generally European aspect but with a large proportion of peculiar species. Wallace asserted that they "confirm the conclusions . . . arrived at from a study of the birds and insects,—that these islands have never been connected with a continent, and have been peopled with living things by such forms only as in some way or other have been able to reach them across many hundred miles of ocean" (IL, p. 256).

The character of the flora of the Azores is also preponderantly that of the southwestern peninsula of Europe, but shows—as does the fauna—a number of endemic species. The facility of seed dispersal across the sea by winds, currents, or transmission by birds readily accounts for the European relationships. The endemism derives from the portion of the present-day flora representing preglacial, and hence more differentiated, immigrants (IL, pp. 260–61). Wallace emphasized that plants—because of their relatively "greater specific longevity and greater powers of endurance under adverse conditions"—afforded the clearest record of the original condition of oceanic islands and of "the primeval immigration" by which they were first stocked (IL, p. 329). The distributional phenomena of the Azores and other oceanic islands established, for Wallace, that they had received different elements of their floras and faunas at different times, but always by means of chance sea-crossings of organisms. Such islands would, he concluded, necessarily house few species of plants and animals in comparison either with continental areas of less favorable environmental conditions or with any islands which had once formed part of a continent.

In marked contrast to oceanic islands are those Wallace

termed "continental islands of recent origin." These are fragments
of continents from which they became separated—by subsidence
of the intervening land—at a relatively recent geological epoch.
Unlike oceanic islands, recent continental islands always contain indigenous land mammals, amphibians, and reptiles. Moreover, the entire flora and fauna of these islands are characterized
by the comparative scarcity of those endemic species and genera
which are so striking a feature of oceanic islands (IL, p. 331).
Great Britain—whose last union with the European mainland,
according to geologists, occurred sometime during the last Ice
Age—is typical of recent continental islands in showing an
almost complete identity in species and genera with its adjacent
mainland. All the indigenous British mammals, amphibians,
and reptiles are identical with those of France and Germany.
British birds, fish, insects, and land-shells, as well as plants, also
agree closely wth those of continental Europe, but present a
number of peculiar species (IL, pp. 370–71).

The distributional phenomena of recent continental islands
were of particular importance as they afforded data for detecting
"the exact process by which nature works in the formation of
species" (IL, p. 357). The varying degrees of endemism on recent
continental islands—ranging from the few peculiar species of
Great Britain to the great number of peculiar species (and some
genera) of Formosa—provided cogent evidence for the role
of geographic isolation in the process of speciation. Geographic
isolation, as is well known, played a crucial part in the genesis
and development of both Wallace's and Darwin's ideas concerning the mechanism by which a parent species gives rise to
one or more daughter species. The large amount of slight variation which constantly occurred in each species, Wallace argued,
was usually prevented from accumulating in any particular direction by the continual intercrossing of the variants with the far
greater parent population in any locality. If a given population
became divided, however, by a barrier which prevents intercrossing, "this tendency to local variation in adaptation to
slightly different conditions, would soon form distinct races"—
incipient species—on either side of the barrier. The sea separating
a newly formed continental island from the mainland is just
such a barrier, and one particularly effective in preventing the

passage of land mammals, amphibians, and reptiles. The longer the separation from the mainland, the greater would be the period of geographic isolation and, hence, modification of insular species. Wallace observed that Great Britain—the most recent of continental islands and one in which "the process of formation of peculiar species has only just commenced"—has, predictably, the fewest endemic species (IL, pp. 408–409). Japan and Formosa, whose separation from Asia occurred long before that of Great Britain from mainland Europe, possess a larger proportion of peculiar species. The distribution and affinities of the flora and fauna of recent continental islands—with their "numerous and delicate gradations in the modification of the continental species, from perfect identity, through slight varieties, local forms, and insular races, to well-defined species and even distinct genera"—present, as Wallace asserted, "an overwhelming mass of evidence in favour of the theory of 'descent with modification'" (IL, p. 410).

Of the third class of islands—"ancient continental"—Wallace considered Madagascar, situated approximately 250 miles from the southeast coast of Africa, the most representative. Like recent continental islands, Madagascar had once been united to its adjacent mainland and would have then received an abundant supply of land animals. But this continental connection was at so remote an epoch—Wallace placed it during the early Eocene (IL, p. 449)—that the animals migrating from Africa were unlike the contemporary inhabitants of that continent. Madagascar preserves, in effect, "the record of a by-gone world,—of a period when many of the higher types had not yet come into existence and when the distribution of others was very different from what prevails at the present day" (IL, p. 411). Besides these elements of an ancient fauna, Madagascar would also have received (owing to the facilities afforded by chance sea transport) successive, though infrequent, immigrations of more modern species from both the west and east. Thus arose, Wallace argued, the complex biota of this "continental island of the first rank, and undoubtedly of immense antiquity" (IL, p. 446).

The most striking aspect of Madagascar's fauna is the large proportion of species and genera peculiar to the island (or allied to remote American or Indo-Asian types) *coupled with* the nearly complete absence of the most characteristic groups of animals now inhabiting Africa (monkeys, apes, lions, zebras, rhinoceroses, and giraffes). This situation follows directly from Wallace's assumption that Madagascar became an island late in the Eocene. Before that break, Madagascar would have received representatives of the fauna then present in Africa: civets, lemurs, insectivores (and other relatively primitive mammals), birds, and reptiles (IL, pp. 416–18). During the period of Madagascar's continental connection, however, (tropical) Africa itself was cut off from any land connection with Europe and Asia by a continuous sea stretching from the Bay of Bengal in the east to the British Isles in the west (GD, I, 286; IL, p. 418). The higher primates and other large mammals, as well as the more highly developed birds, reptiles, and amphibians—which the rich fossil deposits of France, Germany, Greece, and northwest India show to have inhabited the great Palaearctic continent at that period—could not have migrated to tropical Africa. They would, consequently, have been unavailable for colonization of Madagascar. When tropical Africa did become united to the northern land masses in the later Miocene or early Pliocene, Madascar had already lost its land connection to the mainland. It would have been incapable, therefore, of receiving the higher forms of land animals which were then entering and successfully colonizing Africa   (IL, pp. 418-19). This migration from the north led to the reduction or extinction of much of the indigenous African fauna. Secure from the incursion and competition of these higher types—which now constitute Africa's characteristic fauna—Madagascar "was enabled to develop its singular forms of low-type mammalia, its gigantic ostrich-like Æpyornis, its isolated birds, its remarkable insects, and its rich and peculiar flora" (IL, p. 448).

Wallace also claimed that he had dispensed with the hypothesis of an ancient continent stretching across the Indian Ocean—"Lemuria"—which some naturalists had invoked to explain Indian affinities of Madagascar's fauna. The presence of (remotely) allied types of lemurs in Madagascar and India, Ceylon, and the Malay Archipelago was explicable, Wallace argued, simply on their being fragments of an ancient group that had once enjoyed a nearly world-wide distribution but which had subsequently become extinct in most of its former range. The Indian affinities of certain of Madagascar's birds, similarly, require no former land-bridge across the Indian Ocean. Wallace noted that the avian affinities—if ancient—were to be explained as any other case of discontinuous distribution. If, as he thought more likely, the Madagascar and Indian affinities characterized *existing* species and genera, chance overseas migration was the appropriate explanation. Wallace added that the "fact that not one closely-allied species or even genus of [existing] Indian or Malayan mammals is found in Madagascar, sufficiently proves that it is no land-connection that has brought about this small infusion of Indian birds" (IL, pp. 417, 422–27).

New Zealand, an "anomalous island," displayed both oceanic and continental characteristics. Zoologically, it appeared typically oceanic. It possessed no indigenous land mammals and only one endemic amphibian, a frog belonging to the genus *Liopelma* (IL, p. 483). Moreover, its fauna generally showed little close relationship to that of Australia (or any other continent). The geological structure of New Zealand, however, was of a decidedly continental aspect, with ancient sedimentary rocks and abundant deposits of gold, silver, copper, tin, iron, and coal. The presence of a vast submarine bank stretching northwest toward the tropical portion of eastern Australia and New Guinea strongly suggested a former land-connection, and Wallace concluded that New Zealand had once been united to the Australian mainland (IL, pp. 472–74). This union had occurred, however, at a remote epoch when Australia was itself divided (by an ancient sea) into a larger western portion—housing the ancestral forms of the marsupial fauna—and a smaller, faunally impoverished eastern portion (IL, pp. 496–98). This eastern segment —to which alone New Zealand had been united—would not have yet received a mammalian population and would, consequently, have no land mammals available for migration into New Zealand. Those groups which were available for colonization— birds, reptiles, fish, and insects—would, during New Zealand's long subsequent period of insularity, have evolved into its endemic species and genera.

Wallace argued that botanical data supported this analysis of the origin of New Zealand's fauna. The presence of an unusually large number of tropical families and genera of plants in temperate New Zealand follows from its former union having been with the tropical portion of eastern Australia (IL, p. 543). The equally striking absence from New Zealand of the (now) most abundant and characteristic genera of Australian plants—including the *Acacia* and *Eucalyptus*—is explained by their once having been confined, like the marsupials, to the western portion of Australia and thus unavailable for colonization of New Zealand (IL, pp. 490, 499–500). Finally, Wallace opposed any actual land-connection between New Zealand (and Australia) and Antarctica and temperate South America to account for certain faunal and floral similarities. He did concede, however, that a former greater "southern extension towards the Antarctic continent . . . seems . . . probable, as affording an easy passage for the numerous species of South American and Antarctic plants, and also for the identical and closely allied freshwater fishes of these countries" (IL, pp. 485, 521–23).

The publication of *Island Life* marks the completion of Wallace's contribution to biogeography. Although he continued to refine details of his theory, the fundamental principles of geographical distribution had been established. Wallace's synthesis of geological and climatal data, of modes of migration and dispersal of organisms, and of evolutionary adaptation and divergence provided a framework which continues to guide biogeographical studies. That this framework was long held to be inextricably allied to the doctrine of the general permanence of oceanic and continental areas—which Wallace insisted was "the only solid basis for any general study of the geographical distribution of animals [and plants]" (ML, II, 386)—testifies to the power and the scope of his theoretical vision. The degree to which the biogeographical framework must now be loosed from its particular geological moorings is a matter of contemporary scientific analysis. That Wallace made of biogeography one of the most impressive applications of the theory of natural selection is indisputable.

CHAPTER 4

Human Evolution

B OTH Wallace and Darwin had been occupied with the question of human evolution from the start of their respective
careers. However, the wording of the communication to the Linnean Society in 1858 announcing their joint discovery of natural
selection obscures this fact, and the publication of Darwin's *On
the Origin of Species* the following year continued the reticence
on the subject of man. It was Wallace who, in 1864, first aban-
doned that reticence by demonstrating that evolution by natural
selection could provide a comprehensive methodological framework for the scientific study of man. Wallace's writings in the
decade following the publication of the *Origin* are crucial in
understanding his complex—and controversial—interpretation of
the bearing evolutionary theory had upon human concerns. They
provide, moreover, a vivid study of the profound but ultimately
ambiguous role evolutionary theory was to play in the broader
context of Victorian culture.

I *"On the Varieties of Man in the Malay Archipelago"*

Wallace extended the biogeographical arguments he had employed in analyzing zoological distribution in the Malay Archipelago to encompass the human inhabitants of those islands. "On
the Varieties of Man in the Malay Archipelago," read before the
Ethnological Society of London on 26 January 1864, advances the
thesis that the geological history of the Archipelago had a significant influence in determining the character and distribution of
mankind there. Wallace asserted that a line analogous to that
which marks the zoological boundary between the Indo-Malayan
and the Austro-Malayan regions divides the Archipelago into

"two portions, the [human] races of which have strongly marked distinctive peculiarities."[1] That such striking contrasts are found between the Malays (inhabiting the western half of the Archipelago) and the Papuans (inhabiting New Guinea and some adjacent islands) is due to their separate evolutionary histories, the seas dividing the two groups having been far wider in the past than at present. The other groups of natives found among the remaining islands were deemed by Wallace to be "modifications" of the two "primary races" (VM, p. 199).

His protracted intimacy with the Malays and Papuans had enabled Wallace not only to establish their geographical distribution but to specify their racial characteristics in some detail. The "Malay is of short stature, brown skinned, straight haired, beardless, and smooth bodied; the Papuan is taller, is black skinned, frizzly haired, bearded, and hairy bodied; the former is broad faced, has a small nose and flat eyebrows; the latter is long faced, has a large and prominent nose, and projecting eyebrows" (VM, p. 204). Physical traits were not the only criteria adduced to support this classification. Wallace maintained that the racial profiles also included definite behavioral characteristics, moral propensities, and intellectual capabilities. Thus, the Malay is "bashful, cold, undemonstrative, and quiet; the Papuan is bold, impetuous, excitable, and noisy; the former is grave and seldom laughs; the latter is joyous and laughter-loving,—the one conceals his emotions, the other displays them" (VM, pp. 204–205). Finally, the intellect of the Malay was "mediocre" in comparison to the superior mental capacities of the Papuan (VM, pp. 201, 204).

"On the Varieties of Man in the Malay Archipelago" is Wallace's first major extension of the theory of evolution to man himself. Taken in conjunction with "The Origin of Human Races and the Antiquity of Man Deduced from the Theory of 'Natural Selection'" (read before the Anthropological Society on 1 March 1864), "On the Varieties of Man" makes explicit his conviction that anthropological issues were the legitimate concern of the evolutionary biologist—a conviction not entirely popular then. Although the evidence for man's great antiquity was generally accepted by the mid-1860s, resistance was still strong toward a complete explanation of man's nature and history drawn along the strict guidelines of natural selection.[2] Wallace had no such

reservations—although he was soon to alter his position significantly—and drew freely upon all aspects of recent scientific research in offering his version of man's place in nature.

The growing evidence that man's history was to be read in the
long perspective of geological epochs had removed the major
obstacle to the scientific study of the origin and development of
the various human races. Wallace noted that as long as science
"supported the popular belief that man had originated but a few
thousand years ago," it was "impossible to account for the vast
differences observed in mankind by any natural process of
change" (VM, p. 210). A short chronology of human existence
was, simply, too brief to allow for the development of the present
varieties of man from a common ancestor. Archaeological and
paleontological findings of the late 1850s and early 1860s had,
however, dramatically altered the picture. Because man's origin
was now placed at an indefinitely remote period, ethnologists
and anthropologists could

speculate more freely on the parentage of tribes and races. We are
futher enabled to introduce a new element of the greatest importance
into our reasonings on this subject—the geological changes of the
earth's surface; for, as it is now certainly proved that man coexisted
with extinct quadrupeds, and has survived elevations and depressions
of the earth's surface to the amount of at least several hundred feet,
we may consider the effects of the breaking up or re-formation of
continents, and the subsidence of islands, on the migrations, the increase, or the extinction of the people who inhabited them. (VM,
p. 210)

Wallace dismissed the special creationist hypothesis with respect
to man—namely, that the chief human races were "created as they
now are and where they are now found"—just as he had earlier
demonstrated its invalidity in the animal and vegetable kingdoms.
Accordingly, the present distribution and characteristics of races
in the Malay Archipelago are explicable not simply on the basis
of present ecological conditions but by the past geological and
climatal history of those islands. The close resemblance of the
Malays to certain East Asian populations, for instance, argues for
a common origin. Wallace had been particularly struck by the fact
that "when in the island of Bali [he] saw Chinese traders who had

adopted the costume of that country, and who could then hardly
be distinguished from Malays." The evidence from human distribution, moreover, agreed with the pattern of animal distribution
—the same species of large mammalia, for example, inhabit both
the western Malay islands and adjacent portions of the Asian
continent—and reinforced the conclusion that the western islands
"have in all probability formed a connected portion of Asia during
the human period" (VM, p. 211).

The second "primary" race, the Papuan, extends throughout
the eastern part of the Archipelago and as far east as the Fiji
islands. Beyond this, a brown Polynesian population—whose members were practically identical to certain non-Papuan natives
of Gilolo and Ceram (islands near New Guinea) and, except for
the darker color and frizzly hair of the Papuans, quite similar to
the latter—is spread throughout the numerous islands of the
Pacific. Rejecting the argument that these various groups were
simply the result of mixtures, or interbreeding, between several
aboriginal forms—though interbreeding certainly played some role
in human evolution—Wallace insisted that they "are truly intermediate or transitional; and that the brown and the black, the
Papuan, the natives of Gilolo and Ceram, the Fidjian, the inhabitants of the Sandwich Islands and of New Zealand (and perhaps
even of Australia), are all varying forms of one great Oceanic or
Polynesian race" (VM, p. 212).

In explaining the origin and distribution of this Oceanic race,
Wallace relied once more on a juxtaposition of geological and
biological reasoning. He dismissed as unsatisfactory the sugges-
tion that migrations across the oceans from either Asia or the
Americas, in historically recent periods, had populated the Pacific
islands because the Polynesians showed no affinity to the races of
those continents. The hypothesis of "centers of creation" on one
or more of the islands, with subsequent spreading, was also beset
with innumerable objections. Instead, Wallace turned to evidence
supportive of the past existence of an extensive land mass in the
Pacific Ocean. Citing Darwin's *Structure and Distribution of
Coral Reefs* (1842)—a work which demonstrated that the numerous small coral islands (atolls) of the Pacific were produced by
the upward growth of coral on the periphery of land which has
sunk beneath the sea—Wallace argued that the vast Pacific archi-

pelago was "an area of subsidence, and that at a comparatively recent geological epoch wide spreading lands . . . occupied the site of its now thinly scattered islets" (VM, p. 213). Since man was known to have existed at remote periods in the earth's history, there was no difficulty in assuming that there had been human inhabitants of these land masses. After the subsidence of the land masses—which must be distinguished from the hypothetical land-bridges between distant continents which Wallace, by this period, had come to reject—the fragmented populations would be more or less isolated on the remaining atolls and on the volcanic islands (also widespread throughout the Pacific). Given sufficient time and the variability inherent in all organic populations, the original stock would have evolved into the related, but diverse, Polynesian races. Wallace emphasized that his theory rendered unnecessary any supernatural intervention to account for presumed "rapid changes of physical form and mental disposition" (VM, p. 213).

This biogeographical treatment of man was, as Wallace admitted, somewhat speculative and, in parts, based upon inadequate data. Further, as Wilma George has pointed out, man can cross the seas more readily than other mammals; consequently, certain assumptions which are valid in treating the distribution of animals may not be applicable in the reconstruction of human evolution. Wallace's "human line," for example, can not be taken as proving that the Malays came from the West, originally, and the Polynesians from the East. The line—which modern blood group analysis has shown to be an actual boundary between certain human populations, thus lending support to some aspects of Wallace's theory—may mark the eastern limit of one particular wave of colonization from the West. Other western emigrants may have spread further east, giving rise to the races now found in the eastern half of the Malay Archipelago.[3] Despite the questionable nature of certain of Wallace's specific analyses of human distributional patterns, "On the Varieties of Man in the Malay Archipelago" successfully demonstrated that evolution by natural selection could function as a potent explanatory model in the study of man. Wallace's essay, a legitimate product of his belief that "true science only begins when hypotheses are framed to express and combine the facts that have been accumulated"

(VM, p. 215), signaled his entry into the vigorous anthropological debates of the 1860s. Two months later, he was prepared to offer his major contribution to those debates, a contribution which stimulated the evolutionary bias that colored anthropology and Victorian social theory in general.

II The Origin of Human Races

The question of the origin and relation of the several races of man had provoked a controversy in England with profound cultural as well as strictly biological implications. Influenced in part by his reading of Herbert Spencer's *Social Statics* (1850) and his close association with Lyell, Wallace attempted in "The Origin of Human Races and the Antiquity of Man Deduced from the Theory of 'Natural Selection'" (1864) to resolve the dispute between the so-called monogenists and polygenists.[4] The monogenists maintained that man is essentially a single species and that the various races are merely "local and temporary variations, produced by . . . different physical and moral conditions" (OHR, p. clviii). The polygenists argued, in contrast, that the races of man constitute—in effect—separate species, each of which had always been as distinct as it was at present. Both sides had, moreover, produced compelling arguments in support of their respective claims. The monogenists (or "unity" theorists) cited the extensive variations in color, hair, and other features within any given race as proof that each race contains individuals who may be regarded as transitional to other races. This tendency to vary, under the influence of different climates, foods, and habits, would have been sufficient to create, in the long period of human existence, all the present racial differences. The polygenists (or "diversity" theorists) countered that no evidence for any change in the races of man, as far back in time as they could be traced, had ever been brought forward. Paintings and sculptures from the Egyptian tombs, for example, showed that the marked differences between the Semitic and Negro races existed as clearly 5,000 years ago as at present. Wallace, by an ingenious application of the principle of natural selection, effected a compromise between the opposing anthropologists by demonstrating that though racial differences do, in fact, antedate the historical period, the several races ultimately derive from a common ancestor.

According to Wallace's (and Darwin's) theory, animals and plants are always subject to modification by the action of natural selection. When gradually changing environmental conditions make an alteration in an animal's diet or bodily covering expedient, for example, this can be accomplished only by natural selection of appropriate—but randomly occurring— variations in bodily structure and internal organization. But man, Wallace proposed, "by the mere capacity of clothing himself, and making weapons and tools, has taken away from nature that power of changing the external form and structure [in accordance with changes in the external world] which she exercises over all other animals" (OHR, p. clxiii). Sharper spears and better bows substitute for longer nails and teeth, greater bodily strength or swiftness; warmer clothing and better housing substitute for increased bodily hair during glacial epochs. Wallace argued that man, by means of his intellect alone, has been able to respond to environmental demands with an unchanged body. It was the gradual development of mental and moral qualities—particularly the social and sympathetic ones—which, under the influence of natural selection, became the principal avenue of evolution after a certain point in human history. This "great leading idea"—as Darwin described it in declaring it "quite new" to him (ARW, p. 127)— that recent human evolution was (and is) characterized by mental, rather than physical, modification, provided Wallace with a solution to the anthropologists' controversy.

Since the notable and constant physical peculiarities which mark the races of man cannot have been produced or rendered permanent *after* the power of natural selection had begun to operate primarily upon mental variations, they must have existed at an earlier period in human evolutionary history. At this period, when developing man "was gregarious, but scarcely social, with a mind perceptive but not reflective, ere any sense of *right* or feelings of *sympathy*" had appeared, Wallace suggested that it was indeed possible that he existed as a "single homogeneous race without the faculty of speech, and probably inhabiting some tropical region" (OHR, p. clxv). As a dominant species, and one still subject to natural selection of physical variations, early man would have spread throughout the warmer regions of the globe, becoming variously modified according to the exigencies of local conditions. Continued migrations would have exposed different groups to still further extremes of climate, food supply, disease, and natural enemies. Those slight variations in constitution which were either useful in themselves or correlated with useful variations would have been selected and rendered permanent. "Thus," Wallace concluded, "arose those striking characteristics and special modifications which still distinguish the chief races of mankind—[the] red, black, yellow, or blushing white skin; the straight, the curly, the woolly hair; the scanty or abundant beard; the straight or oblique eyes; the various forms of the pelvis, the cranium, and other parts of the skeleton" (OHR, p. clxvi).

While these changes had been occurring, man's mental and moral development would have reached a sufficiently advanced stage to become the principal focus of natural selection. Physical variations would no longer (except in minor instances) be subject to selective action, and the diverse racial characteristics would become fixed, unchanged during the rest of human history. The persistence of these racial characteristics throughout recorded history—"the stumbling-block of those who advocate the unity of mankind"—is not in conflict with the theory of evolution of all races from a common ancestor. As Wallace noted:

If, therefore, we are of [the] opinion that he was not really man till these higher faculties were developed, we may fairly assert that there were many originally distinct races of men; while, if we think that a being like us in form and structure, but with mental faculties scarcely raised above the brute, must still be considered to have been human, we are fully entitled to maintain the common origin of all mankind. (OHR, p. clxvi)

The 1864 essay, which was read with great interest by Spencer and Lyell as well as Darwin (ARW, pp. 277–78), was not restricted to the question of the origin of human races. Rather, Wallace intended it as a vehicle for applying the theory of natural selection to a wide range of anthropological issues. The antiquity of man, as one example, becomes a problem amenable to scientific investigation. The gradual operation of natural selection upon the physical and mental characteristics of developing man would necessitate a long time span for human evolution. Wallace, at this period, was inclined to place the origin of man possibly as far back as the Miocene, noting that we "have no reason to suppose that mind and brain and skull-modification, could go on quicker than that of the other parts of the organisation." It was to a remote age that one had to look to find man in "that early condition" when his mind would have advanced sufficiently to suspend the action of natural selection upon his bodily structure (OHR, pp. clxvi–clxvii). Given the great antiquity of man, it becomes obvious—rather than puzzling—why fossil human crania practically identical to present crania should be found alongside the remains of mammals which have become extinct: man's body would persist unchanged whereas the bodies of other mammals would be subject to continued transformations under natural selection.

Wallace extended the argument to include the contentious issue of racial superiority. He suggested that those races which were exposed to harsher climatic conditions would become hardier, more provident, and more social than the races which lived in subtropical and tropical regions, where food was more abundant and "where neither foresight nor ingenuity are required to prepare for the rigours of winter." Wallace appealed to history to support biology on this point. Claiming that all "the great invasions and displacements of races have been from North to South, rather than the reverse," he cited the successive conquests of the Indian peninsula by races from the Northwest and the conquest of southern Europe by the "bold and adventurous tribes of the North" as proof that the inhabitants of temperate regions are always superior to the races of the tropics. The "great law of '*the preservation of favoured races in the struggle for life*'" operated as inexorably in the human realm as it did throughout the rest of the natural world (OHR, p. clxiv).

Wallace's 1864 essay is notable for its unequivocal declaration of the racial superiority of Europeans. In terminology which he would soon abandon but which was to become commonplace among the more extreme Social Darwinists in the latter decades of the nineteenth century, Wallace averred that natural selection "leads to the inevitable extinction of all those low and mentally undeveloped populations with which Europeans come in contact."

The indigenous populations of North America, Brazil, Australia, Tasmania, and New Zealand succumbed "not from any one special cause, but from the inevitable effects of an unequal mental and physical struggle." Moreover, it is not merely that Europeans are more powerful or more intelligent than other races; they are morally superior. Wallace at this time asserted confidently that the European race—and its descendants—would always conquer the savage races with which it comes in contact "in the struggle for existence, and . . . increase at [their] expense, just as the more favourable increase at the expense of the less favourable varieties in the animal and vegetable kingdoms" (OHR, p. clxv). Despite Wallace's and other leading evolutionists' personal opposition to overt forms of racial discrimination, it is nonetheless clear that their biological concepts and vocabulary could readily be appropriated (however illegitimately) by European and North American racist social theorists.[5]

Wallace further implied that natural selection accounted not only for the superiority of certain races, but also for the preeminent status mankind as a whole held within the animal kingdom. At that period when man's mind had become of greater importance than his bodily structure, "a grand revolution was effected in nature—a revolution which in all the previous ages of the earth's history had had no parallel." Because man could respond to changing environmental conditions by an advance in mental capabilities, Wallace declared that man was in "some degree superior to nature, inasmuch as he knew how to control and regulate her action." Although Wallace was not yet prepared to adduce non-natural causes for man's unique status in the hierarchy of nature, he held that those who maintained that man's attributes argued for a "position as an order, a class, or a sub-kingdom by himself, have some reason on their side" (OHR, p. clxviii). Furthermore, man was not merely at the summit of organic nature; the continued action of natural selection on his intellectual and moral characteristics destined him to an ever higher level of existence. Man's physical well-being would be complemented by an ever-increasing mental and moral evolution, whose nature Wallace described ecstatically in the concluding paragraph of the essay:

Each one will then work out his own happiness in relation to that of his fellows; perfect freedom of action will be maintained, since the well balanced moral faculties will never permit any one to transgress on the equal freedom of others; restrictive laws will not be wanted, for each man will be guided by the best of laws; a thorough appreciation of the rights, and a perfect sympathy with the feelings, of all about him; compulsory government will have died away as unnecessary (for every man will know how to govern himself), and will be replaced by voluntary associations for all beneficial public purposes; the passions and animal propensities will be restrained within those limits which most conduce to happiness; and mankind will have at length discovered that it was only required of them to develope the capacities of their higher nature, in order to convert this earth, which had so long been the theatre of their unbridled passions, and the scene of unimaginable misery, into as bright a paradise as ever haunted the dreams of seer or poet. (OHR, pp. clxix–clxx)

The 1864 essay testifies to Wallace's enduring conviction that the findings of biology—particularly of evolutionary theory—bore directly upon social and political questions. And although he would shortly abandon the position that natural selection alone could account for the origin and development of man and his cultures—or ensure a utopian future—Wallace had constructed a powerful example for the increasing application of biological principles and data to anthropology and Victorian social thought.

III   *Contributions to the Theory of Natural Selection*

Wallace's public position as a foremost proponent of the thesis that man's evolutionary history could be reconstructed solely on the basis of natural selection was altered abruptly in April 1869. In a review of two new editions of geological treatises by Lyell, Wallace announced that man's intellectual capacities and moral qualities—unique phenomena in the history of life—were not explicable by natural selection. Rather, these, as well as certain physical attributes of the human race, required the intervention at appropriate stages of "an Overruling Intelligence" which "guided the action of those laws [of organic development] in definite directions and for special ends."[6] Ironically, it was Darwin's principle of utility that Wallace invoked to substantiate this claim. In the *Origin of Species*, Darwin argued that natural selection could produce neither a structure harmful to an organism nor a structure that was of greater perfection than was necessary for an organism at that particular stage of its evolutionary development.[7] Citing the culture of the "lowest savages"—and, by implication, man at more remote periods in his history—Wallace maintained that the utility principle precluded natural selection as the agent responsible for four of man's characteristic features: the brain, the organs of speech, the hand, and the external form of the body.

The brain of savages, Wallace noted, is of practically the same size and complexity as that of the average European and could, under appropriate cultural conditions, be capable of the outstanding intellectual achievements of civilized man. Yet, the mental requirements of the lowest savages are "very little above those of many animals" and his highly developed brain must be regarded as an organ of greater perfection than necessary for survival. Natural selection which, by the utility principle, could have provided the savage with an intellect only slightly superior to that of the apes, cannot, therefore, be adduced in explaining the complexity of his brain. The hand of the savage is, similarly, an organ of greater refinement than required and could not have been produced by natural selection alone. Furthermore, since man's highest civilized accomplishments—art, science, and technology—were dependent upon "this marvellous instrument," the savage's perfect hand is evidence of provision by a Higher Intelligence of an organ that would be fully utilized only at a later stage in human development.

The erect posture of the savage (and prehistoric man), "his delicate and yet expressive features, the marvellous beauty and symmetry of his whole external form," are additional examples of modifications Wallace claimed were of no physical use to their possessors—indeed, in the case of man's (comparative) nakedness, of possible *disadvantage* in his early history—and are inexplicable by natural selection. Wallace argued, again, for intelligent intervention and provision in the evolutionary process. "The supreme beauty" of the human form and countenance, though initially of no practical use, had (probably) been the cause of man's aesthetic and emotional qualities—which Wallace believed could not have arisen if man had retained the appearance of an erect gorilla. He further suggested that human nakedness, "by developing the feeling of personal modesty, may have profoundly affected our moral nature." The same arguments applied to the complex and delicate physical and mental apparatus responsible for human speech, instruments developed in advance of the needs of their possessors.[8]

The 1869 review concluded with the proposition that a "new standpoint [was possible] for those who cannot accept the theory of evolution as expressing the whole truth in regard to the origin of man." Wallace was careful to declare that the Higher Intelligence, whose action he had invoked to explain that which natural selection could not, was consonant with the teachings of science. Using the analogy of domestic variation—the same analogy he had criticized Darwin for using so extensively in the *Origin*—Wallace stated that just as man had used the laws of variation and selection to produce fruits, vegetables, and livestock, so also "in the development of the human race, a Higher Intelligence has guided the same laws for nobler ends." In both cases, the "great laws of organic development" had been adhered to, not abrogated, and natural selection had been supplemented by conscious selection. In human evolution, Wallace concluded, "an Overruling Intelligence has watched over the action of those laws so directing variations and so determining the accumulation, as finally to produce an organization sufficiently perfect to admit of and even to aid in, the indefinite advancement of our mental and moral nature."[9]

As Malcolm J. Kottler rightly argues, Wallace's volte-face with respect to man was motivated primarily by his growing belief in spiritualism during the period 1865–1869 (see Chapter 5). The utilitarian objections advanced in the 1869 review against the total efficacy of natural selection should not, in themselves, be taken as the basis of Wallace's new position. Rather, they may be read as a scientifically more respectable analysis of the limitations of natural selection than an overtly spiritualist critique would have been. Wallace realized, correctly, that his fellow scientists, with few exceptions, would be unresponsive to—even mocking of—arguments drawn from the then controversial data of psychic phenomena, and he worded his review accordingly. For the next twenty years, he publicly held to the position that a utilitarian analysis was the basis for his critique of natural selection in human evolution, and adduced spiritualism as an explanation for man's unique features only after he had demonstrated the inadequacy of natural selection. The extrascientific origin of his new views is suggested, however, by the fact that he remained throughout the rest of the century the staunchest advocate of the total sufficiency of natural selection as the agent of evolution—except in the case of man—and in his *Darwinism* (1889) even conceded that natural selection could account for the unique physical features of man (though still exempting moral and intellectual qualities).[10]

The 1869 review stands, therefore, as a public watershed in Wallace's career. It was, as Darwin noted, an "inimitably good" exposition of natural selection, but one which concluded with those few remarks on man which made him "groan" (ARW, pp. 199, 206). Wallace, in turn, fully appreciated Darwin's and others' reactions with "regard to my 'unscientific' opinions as to Man, because a few years back I should myself have looked at them as equally wild and uncalled for." Whether Wallace's spiritualist amendments to evolutionary theory fall within the category of scientific or unscientific revisions is a complex question. Within the context of the rich and often ambiguous Victorian philosophies of nature, a demarcation between the two categories is difficult, if not impossible, to fix precisely. In informing Darwin privately that his views on man were "modified solely by the consideration of a series of remarkable phenomena" associated with physical and psychic spirit manifestations, Wallace implied that these "forces and influences [though] not yet recognised by science" would one day be so (ARW, p. 200). That his new opinions had become integral elements in Wallace's biology became clear the following year with the publication of *Contributions to the Theory of Natural Selection* (1870).

Contributions is a collection of ten essays bearing upon various aspects of evolution, the last two of which only will concern us here.[11] The penultimate essay is a basically unmodified reprint of Wallace's 1864 "The Origin of Human Races."[12] Two changes which do appear indicate the extent to which his views on man had shifted. The final euphoric paragraph of the 1864 essay was replaced in the 1870 version by a far more qualified anticipation of the course of human development. Not only did Wallace maintain that the present period of world history was abnormal—the great advances of science often being perverted by "societies too low morally and intellectually to know how to make the best use of them"—but he explicitly rejected the efficacy of natural selection alone in securing any permanent moral or intellectual advance, for it was "indisputably the mediocre, if not the low, both as regards morality and intelligence, who succeed best in life and multiply fastest." Yet Wallace, as so many Victorians, was committed to the belief that mankind was, however erratically, advancing to a more elevated moral and intellectual plateau. As this advance could no longer be ascribed "in any way to 'survival of the fittest,'" Wallace was

forced to conclude that it is due to the inherent progressive power of those glorious qualities which raise us so immeasurably above our fellow animals, and at the same time afford us the surest proof that there are other and higher existences than ourselves, from whom these qualities may have been derived, and towards whom we may be ever tending. (NS, p. 185)

The other significant alteration in the 1870 version is the insertion of the phrase "from some unknown cause" in Wallace's explanation of the great advance in man's mental development at that period in his evolutionary history when his mind, rather than his body, became the major object of natural selection (NS, p. 179). These two changes rendered the 1870 version of the earlier essay inconsistent. Natural selection of random variations was considered, on the one hand, to account for man's unique mental and physical features. But Wallace had interpolated other passages which affirmed the contrary. There was no such ambiguity in the next (and final) essay, written in 1870.

"The Limits of Natural Selection as Applied to Man" elaborates upon the arguments sketched in the 1869 Review and makes explicit Wallace's philosophical commitment to an evolutionary teleology. In rejecting a completely naturalistic version of evolution, Wallace admitted that it will "probably excite some surprise among my readers to find that I do not consider that all nature can be explained on the principles of which I am so ardent an advocate; and that I am now myself going to state objections, and to place limits, to the power of natural selection." Focusing on two phenomena—the origin of consciousness and the development of man from the lower animals—the essay attempts to demonstrate, "strictly within the bounds of scientific investigation," that there exists a providential force responsible for the development of consciousness and those human characteristics which cannot be explained by natural selection (NS, pp. 186–88).

Arguing first from the widely accepted premise that the size of the brain—"universally admitted to be the organ of the mind" (NS, p. 188)—is proportional to mental capacity, Wallace cites evidence from Huxley and the anthropologists Pierre Paul Broca and Sir John Lubbock to show that the brain size of prehistoric man and many of the lowest savages is wholly comparable to that of modern Europeans. This "apparent anomaly" suggests the idea of "a surplusage of power—of an instrument beyond the needs of its possessor" (NS, p. 190). In a harsher portrait than he draws elsewhere in his writings, Wallace depicts

the savage languages, which contain no words for abstract conceptions; the utter want of foresight of the savage man beyond his simplest necessities; his inability to combine, or to compare, or to reason on any general subject that does not immediately appeal to his senses. So, in his moral and aesthetic faculties, the savage has none of those wide sympathies with all nature, those conceptions of the infinite, of the good, of the sublime and beautiful, which are so largely developed in civilised man. Any considerable development of these would, in fact, be useless or even hurtful to him, since they would to some extent interfere with the supremacy of those perceptive and animal faculties on which his very existence often depends, in the severe struggle he has to carry on against nature and his fellowman. (NS, pp. 191–92)

Yet the fact that all the higher intellectual (and moral) faculties do occasionally manifest themselves in the primitive state indicates their latency in the large brain of savage man. That this organ is much beyond his actual requirements is substantiated by the fact that certain of the higher animals, with far smaller brains, exhibit behavioral traits similar, if not identical, to those of the savage. Wallace included in this category the ingenuity of the jaguar in catching fish, the hunting in packs of wolves and jackals, and the placing of sentinels by antelopes and monkeys. The evidence of continuity in psychological and behavioral processes from the higher animals to early man—evidence which provided Darwin with some of the most crucial support for his theory of human evolution by natural causes only—becomes in Wallace's hands testimony that the large brain of savage man was "prepared in advance, only to be fully utilised as he progresses in civilisation." The brain, Wallace concludes, "could never have been solely developed by any of those laws of evolution, whose essence is, that they lead to a degree of organisation exactly proportionate to the wants of each species, never beyond those wants" (NS, p. 193).

The origin of mental faculties such as "the capacity to form ideal conceptions of space and time, of eternity and infinity—the capacity for intense artistic feelings of pleasure, in form, colour, and composition, and for those abstract notions of form and number which render geometry and arithmetic possible," presents equally formidable difficulties (NS, p. 199). The capacity to form abstract ideas, because they lie so "entirely outside of the world of thought of the savage, and have no influence on his individual existence or on that of his tribe," could not have been developed by the accumulation and preservation of gradual mental variations, since such variations would have been of no use in the struggle for existence. That such traits have occasionally been found among certain savage races argues, again, for their future role, not present utility. Wallace claimed this as further testimony to the action of "some other power than the law of the survival of the fittest, in the development of man from the lower animals" (NS, pp. 202–203).

Conscience, or moral sense, is another faculty which Wallace finds problematical according to natural selection. The question of the moral sense—its origin, its psychological force, its relationship to particular criteria of morality—was a complex one in nineteenth-century England. The theory of natural selection, precisely because it sharpened the debate on issues such as the relationship between instinctual and acquired (learned) behavior or between individual and group welfare and survival in nature generally, intensified also the philosophical debates concerning morality. In particular, the connection between man's individual moral sentiments and the social instincts had come under close scrutiny. Wallace's brief statements at this point are merely programmatic—indicating the direction his ethical thought would later follow—rather than sustained critical examinations of the competing schools of British moral philosophy. They reveal, nonetheless, his explicit recognition of the extensive (and perhaps unsettling) extrascientific implications of his and Darwn's theory.

Wallace rejected any utilitarian explanation of the origin of morality, whether of the Benthamite (rational calculation of pleasures and pains) or Darwinist (natural selection of traits for individual or group survival) formulation. He deemed utilitarianism inadequate to account for the peculiar sanctity attached to actions which early man may have considered *moral* as contrasted with the very different feelings with which he regarded what was *useful*. For, even granting that the practice of certain traits, such as benevolence or truthfulness, may have been of use to those tribes possessing them, their moral status and sanctity cannot have been derived from considerations of mere utility. In fact, the utilitarian sanction for truthfulness, Wallace argues, is neither powerful nor universal: its opposite, falsehood, has in "all ages and countries . . . been thought allowable in love, and laudable in war; while, at the present day, it is held to be venial by the majority of mankind in trade, commerce, and speculation." Given the difficulties, practical and otherwise, with which truthfulness has always been beset, and given the many instances in which it has brought "ruin or death to its too ardent devotee," he concludes that considerations of utility could never have invested "it with the mysterious sanctity of the highest virtue,— could [never have induced] men to value truth for its own sake, and practise it regardless of consequences." Wallace advocates, instead, the intuitional theory, which postulates an innate moral sense, antecedent to and independent of experiences of utility. Depending upon individual or racial constitution, and on education and habit—modified by custom, law, and religion—the acts to which its sanction are applied will vary. Most often it is, in fact, those acts of universal utility or self-sacrifice (which are the products of human sympathy and affection) which are deemed moral. But other acts of more dubious worth—"as when the Hindoo will tell a lie, but will sooner starve than eat unclean food, and looks upon the marriage of adult females as gross immorality"—may also receive moral approbation (NS, pp. 200–201). The moral sense, therefore, while essential to the perfect development of man as a spiritual being, cannot be explained on the basis of natural selection.

Discussion of one other human characteristic—relative hairlessness—is of special interest because though seemingly far removed from the preceding arguments leads nonetheless to the same conclusion. One of the most distinctive and universal features of terrestrial mammals is the hairy covering which serves to protect sensitive portions of the skin against the severities of climate, particularly rain. Specifically, Wallace noted that hair is almost invariably directed downward from the upper portions of the body so as to carry off water. Hair, moreover, is least plentiful on those surfaces of the body least exposed to rain and is almost completely absent from the abdominal surface of most mammals. In man, however, the hairy covering has almost totally disappeared and, most remarkably, most completely from the back— one of his more vulnerable surfaces. Wallace asserted that the common habit of savages to use some covering—animal skins or palm leaves, for example—for their shoulders and back (even when they use none on any other part of the body) indicates that they evidently feel the lack of hairy protection and "are obliged to provide substitutes of various kinds" (NS, p. 196). This general absence of hair could have been effected by natural selection only if variations toward hairlessness had adaptive value in the struggle for existence. The evidence points, however, to the contrary case: such variations would have been of no use, or actually disadvantageous, to early man. Natural selection, Wallace concludes, is incompetent to account for man's hairlessness, one more trait which—"by necessitating clothing and houses [and thus leading] to the more rapid development of man's inventive and constructive faculties" (NS, p. 203)—testifies to providential intervention in human evolution.

Wallace closes his critique by turning to the question of the origin of consciousness. Specifically, he is concerned with refuting Huxley's assertion that *"thoughts are the expression of molecular changes in that matter of life which is the source of our other vital phenomena"* (NS, p. 207). Wallace makes a distinction between the ontological status of life—"the name we give to the result of a balance of internal and external forces in maintaining the permanence of the form and structure of the individual"— and consciousness. Whereas life *may* conceivably be regarded as the result of "chemical transformations and molecular motions, occurring under certain conditions and in a certain order," no combination of merely material elements, no matter how complex, could ever produce the "slightest tendency to originate consciousness in such molecules or groups of molecules." Wallace held matter and consciousness to be "radically unlike, exclusive, and incommensurable." Moreover, the presence of consciousness in "material forms is a proof of the existence of conscious beings, outside of, and independent of, what we term matter" (NS, pp. 209–10).

Characteristically, Wallace couches his argument in the language of science. He maintains that Huxley's reductionism is inconsistent with "the most recent speculations and discoveries as to the ultimate nature and constitution of matter" (NS, p. 207). Citing the theory that what is commonly called matter is actually an arrangement of centers of attractive and repulsive force, Wallace asserts that the special properties of matter (electrical, chemical, magnetic) can be explained on the basis of the interaction between these force centers. In repudiating the materialist solution to the problem of consciousness—that all matter is conscious—Wallace declares matter itself to be "essentially force, and nothing but force." Moreover, the various forces in nature— of which matter and consciousness are but different manifestations (Wallace apparently ignores his previous argument on the radical incommensurability of the two)—may be ultimately reducible to "will-force; and thus, ... the whole universe is not merely dependent on, but actually *is*, the WILL of higher intelligences or of one Supreme Intelligence" (NS, pp. 210–12).

Wallace's position at this juncture was (and was to remain) anomalous. He was at once the most effective advocate of natural selection as the primary mechanism of evolution as well as a formidable opponent of a complete evolutionary naturalism. No aspect of evolutionary theory was more sensitive to the play of ideological forces than that which dealt with man, particularly the evolution of his moral and intellectual attributes. The intense public interest and controversy engendered by Darwin's and Wallace's theory of natural selection could hardly have arisen if the question of man's descent from the lower animals was not perceived as an inextricable component of that theory.[13] Wallace's own views on man could scarcely be ignored and "Limits to Natural Selection" drew immediate and heavy criticism. He was chided by both Darwinians, who objected to his spiritualist revisionism—although they could not effectively repudiate all of his scientific arguments on the insufficiency of natural selection—and opponents of evolutionary naturalism, who—while receptive to Wallace's new position on man's origin—felt that he still accorded too great a power to natural selection in the plant and animal kingdoms.[14]

It is instructive at this point to compare Wallace's revision of the theory of natural selection with Darwin's. The first edition of the *Origin of Species* had frankly exposed the difficulties besetting the theory and, as I have noted, Darwin was plagued by these difficulties for the remainder of his life. But his revisions of the theory were always strictly naturalistic in character. His *Descent of Man,* first published in 1871 and thus practically contemporaneous with Wallace's essay, mentions as factors complementary to natural selection the inheritance of acquired characteristics and, most importantly, sexual selection. In conceding the force of Wallace's argument on the harmfulness—or at the least, inutility—of human hairlessness, Darwin invoked sexual selection as the alternative explanation,[15] an alternative rejected by Wallace.[16] And when Darwin states that an "unexplained residuum of change must be left to the assumed uniform action of those unknown agencies, which occasionally induce strongly marked and abrupt deviations of structure in our domestic productions," it seems certain that he assumes those agencies, when known, will fall within the province of natural science.[17] Wallace's "more subtle agencies," in contrast, would seem to require—Wallace, interestingly, terms this a disadvantage in his theory—the "intervention of some distinct individual intelligence, to aid in the production of what we can hardly avoid considering as the ultimate aim and outcome of all organised existence—intellectual, ever-advancing, spiritual man" (NS, pp. 204–205).

In dissociating himself from a complete evolutionary naturalism, Wallace was joining Lyell, Asa Gray, and the larger group of evolutionists—Darwin, Huxley, and the German materialists were among the notable exceptions—who adhered to some type of teleology, however attenuated.[18] His particular version, however, depending as it did on phrenology, psychic phenomena, and spiritualism, was hardly orthodox. As he later wrote, the reality of spiritualist phenomena had first been rejected by him: "All my preconceptions, all my knowledge, all my belief in the supremacy of science and of natural law were against the possibility of such phenomena." It was only when, "one by one, the facts were forced upon me without possibility of escape from them" that Wallace recognized, first, the authenticity of psychic phenomena and, second, after every "other possible solution was tried and rejected" as inadequate, the spiritualist interpretation of them (ML, II, 349). It is within this context that we may understand Wallace's otherwise curious assertion that his critique of natural selection—and its logically distinct, but closely related, spiritualist supplement—in no "degree affects the truth or generality of Mr. Darwin's great discovery" (NS, p. 213), for natural selection still reigned supreme as the mechanism of evolution. And far from upsetting that doctrine—as Darwin had feared (ARW, p. 206)—Wallace devoted the remainder of his long career to establishing the sufficiency of natural selection against the philosophical and scientific objections to it which grew increasingly persistent in the latter decades of the century. By embedding natural selection within the framework of a more general and fundamental law, Wallace argued only that the "laws of organic development have been occasionally used for a special end, just as man uses them for his special ends." It followed—for him—that "natural selection can [not] be said to be disproved, if it can be shown that man does not owe his entire physical and mental development to its unaided action, any more than it is disproved by the existence of the poodle or the pouter pigeon, the production of which are equally beyond its undirected power" (NS, pp. 213–14).

Contributions to the Theory of Natural Selection must be regarded as a crucial document in Wallace's intellectual and professional development. It at once confirmed his position as the articulate champion of natural selection (save, of course, with respect to man's moral and intellectual nature) and signaled the explicit convergence of biological and metaphysical concerns in his evolutionary theory. And though Wallace would continue to maintain an (ostensible) demarcation between them, metaphysical concerns were to influence the subsequent development and elaboration of his scientific, as well as sociopolitical, ideas.

CHAPTER 5

Social and Political Concerns

B Y the 1870s Wallace had come to play a progressively more dominant role in British science. As a participant in the broader process by which European science became increasingly professionalized—and the scientific amateur replaced by the professional scientist—Wallace found himself in an ambiguous position. At that period when a scientist's authority was coming to be defined, at least ostensibly, in terms of his specialized domain of research, Wallace began to speak directly and publicly to those social and political issues which had been obscured in his earlier endeavors. That evolutionary biology, particularly as it bore upon man, was most susceptible to extra-scientific concerns complicated his position. Wallace's explicit quest for cohesive interpretation of human behavior and belief that would be both scientifically accurate and culturally meaningful assumes special importance because of his coauthorship of the biological theory which underlay much of late Victorian thought and action. The intertexture of Wallace's biological and sociopolitical ideas, including spiritualism, land nationalization, and socialism, provides a crucial insight into the ideological complexity of the evolutionary debates on "man's place in nature."

I Spiritualism

During his twelve years of travel in South America and the Malay Archipelago, Wallace had heard of the strange phenomena associated with spiritualism said to be occurring in America and England. Although some of the accounts seemed "too wild and *outré* to be anything but the ravings of madmen," other reports appeared to be well confirmed. Wallace determined, therefore, 122 to ascertain upon his return to London whether the alleged phenomena were legitimate or merely the results of imposture or delusion (ML, II, 276). At first totally skeptical as to the existence of preternatural intelligences, Wallace's early involvement with mesmerism and phrenology nonetheless predisposed him to consider that there might be "mysteries connected with the human mind which modern science ignored because it could not explain."[1] He attended his first séance in the summer of 1865, at the home of a friend, and was impressed with the "rapping and tapping sounds and slight movements of a table" (ML, II, 276). Repeated séances, including several with the renowned English medium Mrs. Marshall later that year, exposed Wallace to a wide variety of physical and mental spirit manifestations. During the following years he continued to attend séances regularly and read voraciously in the spiritualist literature. Satisfied that the tests which he and others devised and executed excluded the possibility of collusion or deception, Wallace gradually became convinced both of the authenticity of these remarkable phenomena as well as of the spiritualist interpretation of them. Accordingly, he set out to overcome the skepticism of the majority of his scientific and literary associates and establish spiritualism as a valid "science of human nature which . . . appeals only to facts and experiment [and which] affords the only sure foundation for . . . the improvement of society and the permanent elevation of human nature" (MMS, pp. 228–29).

Wallace had been struck by the mass of testimony accumulated since the advent of modern spiritualism, which he dated from the reception by the daughters of the Fox family of upstate New York in March 1848 of intelligent communications via "mysterious knockings" (MMS, pp. 152–53). He composed a succinct account of this evidence, which appeared in a secularist journal in 1866 as "The Scientific Aspect of the Supernatural." Wallace prefaced his account by arguing that many events deemed miraculous or supernatural because they appear to run counter to laws of nature are, actually, "natural" and can be shown to involve no violation of natural process, broadly defined (ML, II, 280). To brand certain events incredible because they are inexplicable on then known natural laws, was, Wallace insisted, tantamount to maintaining that man has "complete knowledge of those laws, and can determine beforehand what is or is not possible." The history of science, however, demonstrates the progressive and cumulative character of human knowledge and Wallace noted that "the disputed prodigy of one age becomes the accepted natural phenomenon of the next, and that many apparent miracles have been due to laws of nature subsequently discovered." Five hundred years ago, he declared, the effects produced by the telescope and microscope would have been called miraculous by those ignorant of the laws of optics, just as a century ago "a telegram from three thousand miles' distance, or a photograph taken in a fraction of a second, would not have been believed possible, and would not have been credited on any testimony" (MMS, p. 39). Citing a more closely related and contentious example, Wallace stated that at the start of the nineteenth century the fact that surgical operations could be performed on patients in a mesmeric trance without their apparently "being conscious of pain was strenuously denied by most scientific and medical men in [England], and the patients, and sometimes the operators, denounced as impostors." By the middle decades of the century, however, these phenomena were more generally credited and recognized as a consequence of "some as yet unknown law" (MMS, p. 40). For Wallace, the phenomena of spiritualism—accepted by many but generally ignored or derided by the scientific community—presented an analogous case and could be shown to follow, not contravene, the course of nature.

To render these manifestations "intelligible or possible from the point of view of modern science" required, Wallace suggested, "the supposition that intelligent beings may exist, capable of acting on matter, though they themselves are uncognisable directly by our senses" (MMS, pp. 42–43). The activities of these disembodied intelligences, moreover, were consonant with "the grandest generalisations of modern science, ... [according to which] light, heat, electricity, magnetism, and probably vitality and gravitation, are believed to be but 'modes of motion' of a space-filling ether." That spirits—intelligences of an "ethereal nature"—could act upon ponderable bodies and produce the varied physical effects witnessed at séances was, to Wallace, a legitimate and plausible deduction. Invoking a standard Enlightenment argument that the faculty of vision and existence of light and color would be inconceivable to a race of blind men, Wallace maintained, by analogy, that it is "possible and even probable that there may be modes of sensation as superior to all ours as is sight to that of touch and hearing" (MMS, pp. 44–45).

Wallace's claim was not that the alleged phenomena of spiritualism be accepted uncritically but the more modest one that they be accepted as matters "to be investigated and tested like any other question of science" (MMS, p. 49). The thrust of "The Scientific Aspect of the Supernatural," therefore, depends upon the evidence adduced by "persons connected with science, art, or literature, . . . whose intelligence and truthfulness in narrating their own observations are above suspicion" (MMS, p.53). Wallace was particularly sensitive to the charge that his advocacy of spiritualism was influenced "by clerical and religious prejudice" and detracted from his authority as a student of natural history. He declared that, quite to the contrary, until the time of his first personal acquaintance with the facts of spiritualism he had been a "confirmed philosophical sceptic, rejoicing in the works of Voltaire, [David Friedrich] Strauss [whose influential *Life of Jesus* (1835) denied the supernatural character of Jesus' career and instigated the "higher criticism" of the Bible], and [the German materialist philosopher and zoologist] Carl Vogt." It was not by any preconceived opinions, Wallace asserted, but only "by the continuous action of fact after fact, which could not be got rid of in any other way," that he was "compelled" to accept spiritualism (MMS, pp. vi–vii). He placed great weight upon the testimony of Augustus De Morgan (the English mathematician), Nassau William Senior (the political economist), William Makepeace Thackeray (the novelist), and other eminent figures, each of whom reported witnessing authentic spirit manifestations as diverse as table-moving, communications by raps, clairvoyance, the production of flowers and other objects at séances, and the playing of the "Last Rose of Summer" on an (apparently) unassisted accordion, "but in so wretched a style that the company begged that it might be discontinued" (MMS, pp. 82–87, 95–98).

Although Wallace's main purpose in writing "The Scientific Aspect of the Supernatural" was to encourage skeptical associates to consider the evidence adduced by the advocates of spiritualism with a modicum of objectivity, it was the theoretical and (especially) moral implications of that doctrine which had begun to permeate his "fabric of thought." He concluded his exposition with a brief description of the hypothesis according to which "that which, for want of a better name, we shall term 'spirit,' is the essential part of all sensitive beings, whose bodies form but the machinery and instruments by means of which they perceive and act upon other beings and on matter." At death, the spirit quits the body but still retains "its former modes of thought, its former tastes, feelings, and affections." Wallace claimed that under "certain conditions disembodied spirit is able to form for itself a visible [and, in some instances, tangible] body out of the emanation from living bodies in a proper magnetic relation to itself" and thereby communicate to persons either directly or through the agency of mediums (MMS, pp. 107–10). The significance of these communications, for Wallace, derived not in their imparting any "knowledge to man which his faculties enable him to acquire for himself," but in their moral use: spirit manifestations were incontrovertible evidence of the "reality of another world . . . and of an ever-progressive future state" (MMS, p. 124). He emphasized the continuity between the character of the embodied and disembodied spirit— "in striking contrast with the doctrines of theologians, which place a wide gulf between the mental and moral nature of man in his present and in his future state of existence" (MMS, p. 108) —and chided those critics who scoffed at the trivial nature of some of the events witnessed at séances. Such trivialities, he remarked were hardly "'to be wondered at, when we consider the myriads of trivial and fantastic human beings who are daily becoming spirits, and who retain, for a time at least, their human natures in their new condition" (MMS, p. 110).

The study of spiritualist phenomena seemed, above all, capable of providing insights toward "the partial solution of the most difficult of all problems—the origin of consciousness and the nature of mind" (MMS, p. 114). Wallace maintained that rather than being incompatible with evolution, spiritualism completed his and Darwin's biological theory by accounting for those residual phenomena which—as his 1869 review of Lyell's *Prin-*

ciples and his *Contributions to the Theory of Natural Selection*
would demonstrate—he considered inexplicable by natural selection alone (MMS, pp. vii-viii). Spiritualism was

a striking supplement to the doctrines of modern science. The organic
world has been carried on to a high state of development, and has
been ever kept in harmony with the forces of external nature, by the
grand law of "survival of the fittest" acting upon ever-varying organ-
isations. In the spiritual world, the law of the "progression of the
fittest" takes its place, and carries on in unbroken continuity that
development of the human mind which has been commenced here.
(MMS, p. 116)

Wallace complained, with justification, that the opponents of
spiritualism often refused to investigate the alleged phenomena
or, at most, dismissed them as the result of imposture or delusion
after attending only "two or three chance séances" (MMS,
p. 105). He had 100 copies of "The Scientific Aspect of the Supernatural" printed separately and sent them to those of his colleagues—including Huxley, the physicist and scientific publicist
John Tyndall, and the positivist George Henry Lewes—whom
he hoped to persuade to take up the subject seriously. Tyndall
read the pamphlet "with deep disappointment" and wrote Wallace that, while he saw "the usual keen powers of your mind displayed in the treatment of this question," he deplored Wallace's
willingness to accept data which were "unworthy of [his] attention" (ML, II, 280–81). Huxley, to whom Wallace had described
spiritualism as "a *new branch* of Anthropology," replied that,
although he was "neither shocked nor disposed to issue a Com-
mission of Lunacy against you," he remained completely dis-
inclined to investigate the alleged phenomena (ARW, p. 418).
Huxley's dismissal of the compiled evidence as "disembodied
gossip," which interested him as little as did the more mundane
variety, particularly rankled Wallace and typified the indiffer-
ence or derision with which many of his scientific associates
regarded his efforts (ML, II, 280).

Early in 1874 John Morley, editor of the *Fortnightly Review*,
invited Wallace to contribute an article on spiritualism. General
interest in the movement in England had been quickened by the
investigations and the report of the Committee of the London

Dialectical Society (1871), of which Wallace was a member. He wrote "A Defence of Modern Spiritualism" in a further effort to gain a critical hearing for the experimental claims favoring the reality of the phenomena asserted to be spirit manifestations (ML, II, 295). The hostile reception accorded the psychical experiments of the brilliant chemist and physicist William Crookes —who, while aware of frequent fraudulent practices, had become convinced of the genuineness of certain manifestations, notably those associated with the celebrated Scottish-American medium D. D. Home[2]—reinforced Wallace's belief that the British scientific community maintained an *a priori* antipathy toward the acceptance of positive testimony for spiritualism (MMS, pp. 151, 181–82). In addition to further accounts attesting to various visible and audible phenomena, including the unassisted elevation of the stout medium Miss Nichol (Wallace's protégée) atop the center of a large table, her head just touching the chandelier—an event, given "Miss N.'s size and probable weight," which Wallace deemed unaccountable by "any of the known laws of nature" (MMS, pp. 169–70; ML, II, 292–93)— Wallace described the startling evidence of spiritphotography. First reported in the United States, such photographs were obtained in England from 1872 onwards, commencing with that taken in the presence of Mrs. Guppy (formerly Miss Nichol). Wallace considered them decisive proof of the objective reality of apparitions, settling "the question of the possibility of their being due to a coincident delusion of several senses of several persons at the same time" (MMS, pp. 191–94).

"A Defence of Modern Spiritualism"—together with "The Scientific Aspect of the Supernatural" and a paper Wallace had read before the Dialectical Society in 1871 to induce skeptics to reconsider the question of the inherent credibility or incredibility of miracles ("Miracles: An Answer to the Arguments of Hume, Lecky, and Others, Against Miracles")—was soon reprinted as *On Miracles and Modern Spiritualism* (1875). The volume sold well, going into a third edition in 1896, and Wallace regarded it as having persuaded "many persons to investigate the subject and to become convinced of the reality of the phenomena" (ML, II, 295). Wallace emphasized that his purpose at this stage was not to promulgate the teachings of spiritualism but to demonstrate the validity of its alleged phenomena:

> My position, therefore, is that the phenomena of Spiritualism in their entirety do *not* require further confirmation. They are proved quite as well as any facts are proved in other sciences; and it is not denial or quibbling that can disprove any of them, but only fresh facts and accurate deductions from those facts. When the opponents of Spiritualism can give a record of their researches approaching in duration and completeness to those of its advocates, and when they can discover and show in detail either how the phenomena are produced or how the many sane and able men here referred to have been deluded into a coincident belief that they have witnessed them, and when they can prove the correctness of their theory by producing a like belief in a body of equally sane and able unbelievers—then, and not till then, will it be necessary for spiritualists to produce fresh confirmations of facts which are, and always have been, sufficiently real and indisputable to satisfy any honest and persevering inquirer (MMS, pp. 211–12).

Wallace's persistent assertions that his conversion to spiritualism was prompted initially by experimental evidence, obtained by himself and others (MMS, pp. 126–44), pose the question of his competence as a critical investigator of the phenomena witnessed at séances and elsewhere. The verdict of many of his contemporaries that his trusting disposition and unfailing confidence in the essential goodness of man—which withstood "even losses of money and property incurred through this faith in others' virtues" (ARW, p. 354)—rendered him gullible with respect to the evidence for psychic phenomena cannot be dismissed entirely. Wallace, characteristically, put the onus of proof upon the detractors of séances, declaring that "nine-tenths of the alleged frauds in mediums arise from the ignorance of the sitters" (ARW, p. 437). His vigorous defense of mediums, including testifying in court, surprised even some supporters of spiritualism. Frederick Myers, a leading late Victorian psychical researcher, felt that Wallace's "worst credulity as to the good faith of cheating mediums belongs to a separate compartment of his mind—or rather forms a part of his innocent generosity of nature, an unwillingness to believe that anyone will do anything wrong."[3]Notwithstanding these assessments, it seems clear that, unless one is prepared to reject the entire mass of testimony for the authenticity of spirit manifestations, at least some of Wallace's psychical experiences must be divorced from charges of hallucination or trickery.[4] Carl Jung's comment on Wallace in this context is judicious. Noting that even if the spiritualist interpretation of the observed psychical facts be disputed, Jung asserted that Wallace—along with Myers, Crookes, and the Cambridge philosopher Henry Sidgwick—merited praise for "having thrown the whole of [his] authority on to the side of non-material facts, regardless of . . . the cheap derision of [his] contemporaries; even at a time when the intellect of the educated classes was spellbound by the new dogma of materialism, [Wallace] drew public attention to phenomena of an irrational nature, contrary to accepted convictions."[5]

It is against this background of rising scientific naturalism in the second half of the nineteenth century that Wallace's deepening commitment to spiritualism is best understood. Wallace was one of a small but significant group of thinkers for whom both traditional Christianity and the concepts of Victorian science were incapable of providing adequate guidelines for a holistic philosophy of man. Convinced from an early age that dogmatic Christianity was ethically questionable and morally ineffective (ML, II, 53–54; ARW, p. 414), Wallace's growing disenchantment during the 1860s with the pretensions of the advocates of scientific naturalism to prescribe acceptable codes for human behavior or guarantees of ultimate purpose led him to pursue a path that lay between science and orthodox religion. The metaphysical and ethical teachings of spiritualism, combined with those of phrenological psychology (whose emphasis upon irreducible mental and moral faculties was consistent with Wallace's new views on human evolution), appealed to him because they provided an experimentally based explanation for the past and future development of moral and intellectual nature and subsumed man's total being under a consistent cosmic law.[6] Unlike what he considered the artificial character of Christian ethics, with its "arbitrary system of rewards and punishments dependent on stated acts and beliefs only," spiritualism's "system of natural and inevitable reward and retribution, dependent wholly on the proportionate development of our higher mental and moral nature, . . . is in harmony with the whole order of nature." Man would be "impelled towards a pure, a sympathetic, and an intellectual life" and be deterred from base or selfish behavior, Wallace affirmed, by the knowledge that the latter habits entailed "future misery, necessitating a long and arduous struggle in order to develop anew the faculties whose exercise long disuse has rendered painful to him." It was the loftiness of its doctrines coupled with the immediacy of those phenomena which bring "home to the mind even of the most obtuse the absolute reality of [a] future existence" that constituted, for Wallace, spiritualism's valid claim to the status of moral science (MMS, pp. 224–25).

From the 1880s onward, Wallace became less actively involved in spiritualist causes. With the exception of his membership in the newly formed (1882) Society for Psychical Research and his enthusiastic attendance at séances in Boston, Washington, and San Francisco during a lecturing tour in the United States in 1886–1887 (ML, II, 337–49), his interest in spiritualist concerns was confined primarily to private correspondence and contributions to various periodicals. Moreover, aside from some comments in the final chapter (on man) in *Darwinism* (1889), Wallace largely kept his spiritualist convictions from intruding into his scientific writings of the closing decades of the century. That these convictions, however, had become constitutive in the emerging fabric of his scientific, as well as sociopolitical, theories is indisputable. Although an explicit Weltanschauung—an evolutionary teleology in which science and spiritualism finally merged—would await the publication of *Man's Place in the Universe* (1903) and *The World of Life* (1910), the moral and philosophical tenets of spiritualist doctrine informed Wallace's meliorist crusades and his critique of Victorian technological civilization.

II Land Nationalisation (*1882*)

Wallace's early introduction to radical social and political speculation, primarily through the writings and teachings of the

Socialist Robert Owen, instilled in him a critical attitude toward central maxims of British legislation and political economy (ML, I, 89). The years spent in land-surveying, prior to the voyage to South America, provided him with a detailed knowledge of the laws and practices governing private and public property, although he did not at that period in his life consider those laws egregiously unjust or unwise (ML, I, 158). It was a reading of Spencer's *Social Statics* (1850)—particularly the chapter on "The Right to the Use of the Earth"—upon his return from the Amazon which exerted a decisive influence in turning Wallace's interests toward social and political reform (ML, II, 235). His travels in the Malay Archipelago were undertaken, consequently, with a heightened attention to anthropological and sociological, in addition to strictly biological, data. Wallace's prolonged residences in primitive communities both in South America and the East compelled him to question whether Europe had, in fact, attained that pinnacle of social and moral development which its undoubted scientific and material progress seemed to render axiomatic to many Victorians.

During these travels, Wallace had been repeatedly struck by the "remarkable [fact] that among people in a very low stage of civilization we find some approach to . . . a perfect social state [in which] . . . there are none of those wide distinctions, of education and ignorance, wealth and poverty, master and servant, which are the product of our civilization" (MA, II, 460). He concluded *The Malay Archipelago*, somewhat startlingly, with a denunciation of the highly vaunted civilization of nineteenth-century Europe. Technical mastery over the forces of nature had indeed brought about a vast accumulation of wealth and an ever more prodigious international commerce. It had also, Wallace asserted, brought about those crowded towns and cities which "support and continually renew a mass of human misery and crime *absolutely* greater than has ever existed before" (MA, II, 462). Of the several examples which he adduced to argue that it was European man—rather than the so-called savages among whom he had lived—who suffered under a "barbaric" social and moral organization, Wallace specified the abuses engendered by private property:

We permit absolute possession of the soil of our country, with no legal rights of existence on the soil, to the vast majority who do not possess it. A great landholder may legally convert his whole property into a forest or a hunting-ground, and expel every human being who has hitherto lived upon it. In a thickly-populated country like England, where every acre has its owner and its occupier, this is a power of legally destroying his fellow-creatures; and that such a power should exist, and be exercised by individuals, in however small a degree, indicates that, as regards true social science, we are still in a state of barbarism. (MA, II, 464)

These passages in *The Malay Archipelago*, the most popular of all his books, mark Wallace's debut as a social critic, a role he was to exercise with increasing fervor. John Stuart Mill, impressed with Wallace's sentiments, asked him to become a member of the General Committee of his proposed Land Tenure Reform Association. The association, whose main object was to claim for the state all future unearned increment of land values—the increase in land value *not* deriving from any actual improvements by the owner—was formed in 1871, and Wallace attended its meetings until Mill's death in 1873 caused its dissolution (ML, II, 235, 238). The question of land reform continued to occupy Wallace intermittently for the next several years, but he was deterred from offering any definite proposals for nationalization by the objections to it advanced by Mill, Spencer, and their followers. They, while severe critics of the inequities of private property in the land, opposed any reform which would entail what they regarded as a pernicious increase in state intervention. The bitter controversy over Irish landlordism which intensified during 1879–1880 drew Wallace once again into the agitation for land reform. The ineffectualness of the proposals put forward convinced him that state ownership of some kind was essential to remove the abuses of the existing land-tenure system, and it now occurred to him that there was a method which would obviate the major objections to nationalization.

All land, Wallace proposed, would revert to the state while the improvements or increased value given to the land—such as buildings, drains, plantations—would remain the salable property of the present owner (now "state-tenant"). The management of the land, therefore, would devolve not to the state but to the actual tenant proprietors. The publication of these views in an article in the *Contemporary Review* (November 1880) immediately attracted the attention of those who desired land reform but opposed increased state intervention in land management. The Land Nationalization Society, with a program based on Wallace's principles, was formed in 1881 with Wallace as its president (ML, II, 239–40). *Land Nationalisation: Its Necessity and Its Aims* was published the following year.[7]

Wallace dedicated *Land Nationalisation* to "the working men of England" and intended it as a rigorous yet easily comprehensible demonstration that "the vast riches and the degrading poverty of [England], which, in their terrible combination and contrast, are unparalleled in the civilised world" derive from its system of land tenure (LN, p. 176). Drawing upon a mass of documentary evidence, including the reports of Parliamentary Commissions, Wallace argued that private ownership in land necessarily produces evil results "of the most alarming magnitude" (LN, p. 134). Moreover, the widespread pauperism, vice, and crime of large portions of the English laboring classes—"which strike foreigners with the greatest astonishment" (LN, p. 176)—are due not to any special ignorance or ill-conduct on the part of English landlords but are inherent in the system itself (LN, p. 135). Wallace declared that so long as the "highest teaching of political science" tells the great landlords "that their land is their *property*," they will necessarily act so as to increase the profits from their holdings (LN, pp. 178–79). And every step taken to secure this end—whether it be the enclosure of common land, the eviction of tenants from their homes to convert farms into game preserves or smaller holdings into larger ones, or the outright appropriation of the added value given to the land by the labor of tenants—is, Wallace noted ironically, "supported by the power and majesty of the law" (LN, p. 135). The fact that many landholders were also magistrates further enhanced their power to coerce their tenants into conformity with their own political and religious opinions. Wallace added to this catalogue of despotic powers over individuals—"such as we are accustomed to look upon with horror when occurring in the Turkish or Russian Empires" (LN, p. 100)—the right of English landlords, as absolute owners of the land, to destroy ancient monuments and to work, sell, export, and totally exhaust the (nonrenewable) mineral wealth of the country solely for individual profit without regard for the national interest or future generations (LN, pp. 129–32).

In contrast to the miserable condition of many of the agricultural and town laborers of England (and Scotland and Ireland), Wallace cited contrary examples from Switzerland, Germany, Norway, Belgium, France, and the United States. In those countries, the system of "occupying ownership"—whereby the occupier and cultivator of the land is also its owner—though not universal, was widespread and the population generally satisfied and thriving (LN, pp. 137, 182–83). Wallace concluded that "in order to effect a real and vital improvement in the condition of the great mass of the English nation, not only as regards physical well-being, but also socially, intellectually, and morally," a radical change in the system of land tenure was required. Only if private ownership of the land as a source of income from its rent or for commercial speculation were abolished, and each cultivator of the land became its virtual, but not absolute or unrestricted, owner, would England possess the "healthy, moral and contented" population its great wealth would seem to permit (LN, pp. 18–19).

Wallace emphasized that any reform which merely transferred absolute ownership of the land from existing landlords to existing tenants would be self-defeating. The new owners, being free to divide their holdings and sublet portions, would in time constitute a new privileged class and the worst abuses of landlordism would revive. Wallace's fundamental conviction that every citizen be given the opportunity to procure suitable land for his personal occupation—with permanent security of tenure—entailed that the state alone be the actual owner of the land and that subletting be prohibited by law. His proposal for land nationalization necessitated that a "person must own land only so long as he occupies it personally; that is, he must be a perpetual *holder* of the land, not its absolute *owner*" (LN, p. 193).

To effect the transfer to state ownership, Wallace proposed a Land Nationalization Act predicated upon the distinction he had earlier drawn between the inherent value of the land (depending on natural conditions such as geological formation, climate, aspect, surface, and subsoil) and the improvements added to the inherent value by the labor or outlay of the owners or occupiers. Upon the date of the act's coming into operation, the state would assume ownership of the land and would be remunerated for its use by payment of an annual "quit-rent," determined according to the assessed inherent value of each plot. The improvements which had been created by the exertions of the landholders (or their predecessors) would remain their absolute property and would henceforth constitute the "tenant-right," to be retained by them or sold as they wished. Wallace was opposed to outright confiscation of landed property and proposed that each existing landowner, and "any heir or heirs of the landowner who may be living at the passing of the Act, or who may be born at any time before the decease of the said owner," be paid an annuity by the state equal to the same net income from the land derived prior to nationalization (LN, p. 199). He defended this temporary continued "existence [of] a class of pensioned idlers, living upon the labours of others, without the smallest exertion of body or mind on their own part," on the grounds that the property of living individuals (and their immediate heirs) be strictly respected by the state (LN, p. 198). Future descendants, Wallace declared, had no such proprietary rights to the land (exclusive of tenant-right). He considered the presumed rights of inheritance one of the worst abuses of landlordism.

Existing tenants at the time the Nationalization Act took effect would be entitled to continue the occupation of their houses or farms upon payment to the state of the annual quit-rent. Each tenant also would have to acquire the tenant-right to the property, by purchase from the existing landlord. As absolute owner of the tenant property, he would then be free, if he chose, to sell or bequeath either all or part of it. For those unable to provide the sum necessary for purchase of the tenant-right, Wallace suggested that loan societies or municipal authorities be empowered to advance the required sum, which would then be repaid by the tenant over some fixed length of time (LN, p. 202). Wallace insisted that such mortgaging be strictly limited to prevent anyone from undertaking to farm more land than his capital and abilities warranted, that is, from farming under a perpetual mortgage. At the same time, there need be no upper limit to the extent of land any single state-tenant could occupy. A wealthy individual might retain or purchase rights to a vast acreage. Since he could not sublet any portion of his tenant-right, however, Wallace envisioned no reason for anyone retaining more land than he and his daily employees could feasibly operate. City dwellers who so chose could also exercise the universal right embodied in Wallace's program and select plots of available agricultural land or portions of commons or waste lands for their personal occupation in proximity to cities and towns. Such (presumably) salubrious dwelling-places would, he maintained, "always produce health and contentment" and would, for those industrial workers who utilized their land only to produce food as a supplement to purchased provisions, provide some security in times of unemployment. Finally, Wallace suggested—but did not specify how—urban residences be similarly nationalized, and the present occupiers of leasehold houses or rental premises enabled to become their owners (LN, pp. 205–18).

The publication of *Land Nationalisation* secured Wallace a prominent role in the public debate on land reform, a debate which during the late 1870s and 1880s provided a major focus for the broader question of social and political reform in Great Britain.[8] Wallace's new role did not, as Darwin feared, force him to "turn renegade to natural history" (ARW, p. 262). Rather, Wallace would continue to probe more critically the relationship of evolutionary biology to sociopolitical issues. As Robert M. Young has pointed out, it "is not in the least surprising that those who were interested in the relationship between man and nature should, with consistency, be concerned about workers and property, and conversely."[9] Just as Wallace had earlier reassessed the operation of natural selection in human evolution, he would now analyze the use (or misuse) of his and Darwin's theory to buttress particular social and economic policies. His views on land nationalization must be seen as integral elements in what may be termed Wallace's unorthodox Social Darwinism, in which biological and Socialist convictions reacted upon one another. While writing *Land Nationalisation*, Wallace had read *Progress and Poverty* (1879) by the radical American economist Henry George. George's thesis that material progress had engendered rather than alleviated human poverty and misery paralleled Wallace's own claims. He regarded George's work as providing "a most remarkable theoretical confirmation" of the inductive argument he had developed in examining the evidence of the actual condition of people under different systems of land tenure (LN, p. 173). Wallace was particularly struck by George's devastating critique of the Malthusian schools of political economy. He informed Darwin that George, who accepted the operation of Malthus's principle of population with respect to animals and plants, denied that "it ever has operated or can operate in the case of man, still less that it has any bearing whatever on the vast social and political questions which have been supported by a reference to it" (ARW, p. 260). Of course, Wallace—who maintained that natural selection had been operant in the development of man's physical and certain of his mental attributes—rejected George's disavowal of evolutionary biology with respect to human questions. He was fully sympathetic, however, to George's arguments against laissez-faire economic policies. His own critique of competitive capitalism, implicit in *Land Nationalisation*, would develop in the coming decade into an overt espousal of socialism and a polemicized social biology.

III *Socialism*

During the years immediately following his initial public advocacy of land nationalization, Wallace was inclined to think that no more radical reform would be necessary to divest society of the abuses of unregulated private ownership of property. His early interest in Owenite socialism had been tempered "by the individualistic teachings of Mill and Spencer, and the loudly proclaimed dogma, that without the constant spur of individual competition men would inevitably become idle and fall back into universal poverty." In 1889 this philosophical and political tension was resolved finally by a reading of Edward Bellamy's staid but influential Socialist utopian *Looking Backward* (1888), which Wallace regarded as a definitive repudiation of every "sneer, every objection, every argument [he] had ever read against socialism." "Human Selection," published in the *Fortnightly Review* the following year (1890), is both Wallace's first public declaration as a Socialist and his "first scientific application of [that] conviction" (ML, II, 266–67).

Wallace, as I have indicated, allowed natural selection a great but circumscribed role in the development of man, particularly in the development of certain of his mental faculties. "Human Selection" is his most explicit statement with respect to that complex of arguments which, by the closing decades of the century, had coalesced into a confused, contradictory, but always culturally potent Social Darwinism. Wallace began by noting that in "one of my latest conversations with Darwin he expressed himself very gloomily on the future of humanity, on the ground that in our modern civilization natural selection had no play, and the fittest did not survive. Those who succeed in the race for wealth are by no means the best or the most intelligent, and it is notorious that our population is more largely renewed in each generation from the lower than from the middle and upper classes."[10] Although less sure of the mental or moral superiority attributed to those segments of the population enjoying a privileged ranking in the social and political hierarchy than perhaps Darwin was, Wallace agreed that there was an undoubted check to progress in social evolution.

He dismissed as possible solutions to this evolutionary dilemma any proposals based solely upon beneficial environmental influences, such as education or hygiene. Though these could obviously produce improvements in any given generation, Wallace held that they could not of themselves lead to a sustained improvement of humanity. Implicit in such proposals was "the belief that whatever improvement was effected in individuals was transmitted to their progeny, and that it would be thus possible to effect a continuous advance in physical, moral, and intellectual qualities without any selection of the better or elimination of the inferior types" (SSS, I, 510). The inheritance of acquired characteristics was accepted by many evolutionists—Darwin always conceded some efficaciousness to its presumed influence—and, under the rubric of neo-Lamarckianism, underlay certain biologically oriented reformist speculations in the 1880s and 1890s.[11] Wallace considered, however, that the researches of Francis Galton and of August Weismann, in particular, had demolished the theory of the inheritance of acquired traits. According to Weismann, the hereditary material (germ-cells in the ovaries and testes which produce egg and sperm) cannot be modified by changes undergone by the remaining body cells (comprising the somatoplasm).[12] Wallace accepted Weismann's influential but controversial hypothesis and concluded that there remained "some form of selection as the only possible means of improving the race" (SSS, I, 510).

Wallace rejected, however, what he termed artificial selection, under which he included such schemes as Galton's eugenics. Among Galton's proposals was "a system of marks for family merit," whereby those individuals who rated well in health, intellect, and morals would be encouraged—by state subvention —to marry early and raise large families. While such positive eugenics might increase slightly the number of excellent human specimens, Wallace argued that it would be socially ineffective and evolutionarily insignificant as it would leave the bulk of the population unaffected and fail to "diminish the rate at which the lower types tend to supplant . . . the higher" (SSS, I, 513). Given the limited knowledge of human inheritance, Wallace maintained that artificial selection was not only scientifically dubious, but culturally pernicious. Eugenics, by perpetuating class distinctions, would postpone social reform and afford quasi-scientific excuses for keeping people "in the positions Nature intended them to occupy." Negative eugenics, or the prevention or discouragement of procreation by those deemed unfit, seemed to Wallace "a mere excuse for establishing a medical tyranny. And we have enough of this kind of tyranny already . . . the world does not want the eugenist to set it straight. . . . Eugenics is simply the meddlesome interference of an arrogant scientific priestcraft" (ARW, pp. 466–67).

For Wallace, neo-Lamarckianism, eugenics, and individualistic Social Darwinism were not merely biologically questionable; they also proceeded from a fundamentally objectionable social premise. All such schemes, he maintained, were predicated upon class distinctions and economic inequities (in greater or lesser degree). As such, they ignored or failed to confront the central fact that Victorian capitalism frustrated, rather than facilitated, the operation of that biological selection which he insisted was the sole mechanism for permanent human evolutionary advance. Socialism, in contrast, would provide the sufficient—and necessary (ML, II, 266)—condition for progress:

[W]hen we have cleansed the Augean stable of our existing social organization, and have made such arrangements that *all* shall contribute their share of either physical or mental labour, and that all workers shall reap the *full* and equal reward of their work, the future of the race will be ensured by those laws of human development that have led to the slow but continuous advance in the higher qualities of human nature. When men and women are alike free to follow their best impulses; when idleness and vicious or useless luxury on the one hand, oppressive labour and starvation on the other, are alike unknown; when all receive the best and most thorough education that the state of civilization and knowledge at the time will admit; when the standard of public opinion is set by the wisest and the best, and that standard is systematically inculcated on the young; then we shall find a system of selection will come spontaneously into action which will steadily tend to eliminate the lower and more degraded types of man, and thus continuously raise the average standard of the race. (SSS, I, 517)

Socialism, by removing disparities of wealth and rank, would foster the selection of reproductive partners based not upon economic or political factors, but upon a concern solely for those eminent moral, intellectual, and physical characteristics which often were neglected (or rendered subservient) in capitalist-competitive society (SSS, I, 526).

That the selective process Wallace envisioned as the key to further human evolution is a form of sexual selection is, at first sight, surprising. One of the major theoretical disagreements between Wallace and Darwin had stemmed precisely from Wallace's refusal to accord scientific status to female choice as an agent of evolution. In the *Origin*, Darwin had briefly introduced the theory of sexual selection to account for certain animal characteristics whose occurrence did not seem explicable on the basis of natural selection. Specifically, "when the males and females of any animal have the same general habits of life, but differ in structure, colour, or ornament," Darwin argued that such sexual dimorphism arose not from "a struggle for existence, but [from] a struggle between the males for possession of the females." He further indicated that sexual selection includes two distinct processes. First, in certain species, particularly polygamous ones, there is an actual (or threatened) combat between males for the privilege of coition. Those males possessing variations which better equip them for combat will succeed in competition with their rivals and leave the most progeny (who inherit those variations). Thus, Darwin suggested, arose the antlers of male deer, the spurs on the legs of certain male birds, and the huge mandibles of male stag-beetles. Second, there are species in which the males possess musical organs, bright coloration, or ornamental appendages (such as the elaborate tails of the male birds of paradise). Darwin claimed that such traits had developed because the females were more attracted to males of striking appearance, adding that he saw "no good reason to doubt that female birds [for example], by selecting, during thouands of generations, the most melodious or beautiful males, according to their standard of beauty, might produce a marked effect."[13]

Initially, Wallace conceded some evolutionary role to sexual selection. He agreed with Darwin that male rivalry—which Wallace designated "a form of natural selection which increases the vigour and fighting power of the male animal, since, in every case, the weaker are either killed, wounded, or driven away" (D, p. 282)—was an actual mechanism for evolution. Throughout his career, Wallace maintained that to male rivalry must be imimputed "the development of the exceptional strength, size, and activity of the male, together with the possession of special offensive and defensive weapons" (D, p. 283). However, the second part of Darwin's hypothesis, female choice, struck Wallace as dubious at the least (ARW, p. 130; ML, II, 18). Two essays on animal coloration which appeared in 1867—"Mimicry, and Other Protective Resemblances among Animals" and "On Birds' Nests and Their Plumage"—reveal the degree to which Wallace had come to differ from Darwin.[14]

Among the more curious modifications of the coloring and external form of animals are those instances when one species resembles another unrelated species so closely as to make it difficult to distinguish between them (by appearance). It was Wallace's friend and co-explorer Bates who, in 1862, first explained such imitation—which he termed mimicry—on the principle of natural selection. During his travels in South America, Bates had noticed that the brilliantly-hued heliconid butterflies of the Amazon region were copied both in color and pattern by several unrelated species, including the Leptalides (*Dismorphia*) butterflies. Because the Heliconidae secrete substances (with nauseous odors) which render them unpalatable to insectivorous birds—and are thus avoided as prey—Bates reasoned that the mimicking butterflies (which lack the offensive secretions) acquire protection merely by looking like the original. Natural selection, he argued, would favor just those variations which more closely approximated the appearance of the protected species, "the selecting agents being insectivorous animals, which gradually destroy those sports or varieties that are not sufficiently like [the Heliconidae] to deceive them." Over time, cumulative selective pressure would result in the production of those remarkable insects which exactly resemble (externally) the model species. Both Darwin and Wallace recognized Bates's explanation as providing powerful empirical support for their theory and Wallace explicitly endorsed Batesian mimicry in 1865 in his important essay "On the Phenomena of Variation and Geographical Distribution as illustrated by the *Papilionidae* of the Malayan Region."[15] Two years later, in his article on mimicry in the *Westminster Review*, Wallace extended Bates's idea to incorporate the widespread phenomena of protective resemblances (in general) among animals within the evolutionary framework.

Invoking the principle of utility, Wallace argued that many aspects of the coloration and external appearance of animals—including traits hitherto regarded as useless or trivial by naturalists—are (or were), in fact, often of the utmost importance for survival (NS, pp. 35–36, D, pp. 134–35). The diverse instances of resemblance, whether to the surrounding environment or to other animals, are evolutionary adaptations which serve either to conceal creatures from their predators or from those animals they themselves prey upon. Wallace cited the green-plumed groups of tropical birds (such as the parrots, barbets, and touracos), the many dusky nocturnal creatures (including rats, bats, and moles), the polar bear, the arctic fox, the alpine hare, and the "flounder and the skate, [which] are exactly the colour of the gravel or sand on which they habitually rest," as affording evidence of such adaptive coloration (NS, pp. 36–41). The so-called "walking-stick insects" of the family Phasmidae provide a particularly striking example in that their coloring, external form and texture, and the arrangement of the head, legs, and antennae cause them to be identical in appearance to the twigs and branches on which they rest (NS, pp. 46–47). Wallace claimed that all such traits—"from the mere absence of conspicuous colour or a general harmony with the prevailing tints of nature, up to such a minute and detailed resemblance to inorganic or vegetable structures as to realise the talisman of the fairy tale, and to give its possessor the power of rendering itself invisible" (NS, p. 47) —are explicable on the same laws of rapid multiplication, incessant slight variation, and natural selection which govern other evolutionary modifications (NS, p. 49). Batesian mimicry becomes, accordingly, merely a special case of protective coloration and one, Wallace suggested, which may include not only insects, but snakes and birds as well (NS, pp. 70–76).

The 1867 essay concluded with a brief—but significant—discussion of the relation of protective coloring and mimicry to the sexual differences of animals. For those species of insects (and birds) in which the sexes are dissimilar in color or marking, Wallace suggested that the generally duller and less conspicuous coloration of the females was an adaptation which served to conceal them from predators during the depositing of eggs. "In the spectre insects (Phasmidae)," he noted, "it is often the females alone that so strikingly resemble leaves, while the males show only a rude approximation" (NS, p. 79). Conversely, those insects with little need for protective concealment, such as the Heliconidae and the stinging Hymenoptera (wasps, bees, ants), display no (or only slightly-developed) sexual differences in color. Wallace regarded the general absence of color differentiation between the sexes in species of insects protected by "disagreeable flavour, . . . by their hard and polished coats, [or by] their rapid motions" as compelling evidence against the hypothesis of female choice. Although he did not completely abandon sexual selection—which "has often manifested itself [among insects] by structural differences, such as horns, spines, or other processes"—Wallace's analysis of the development and function of color in the animal kingdom foreshadows the increasing commitment he would make to natural selection as the major agency of evolution (NS, p. 80).

The "Theory of Birds' Nests" developed further the thesis that the dull coloration of females in many species is due, not to selection by the females of more handsomely colored males, but to their greater need for concealment. Wallace claimed that birds, because of their prolonged period of incubation, provided a decisive support for his own hypothesis. In the majority of cases in which male birds are more brilliantly colored, he noted that the female hatched the young in open nests. During brooding, the female would be "exposed to the attacks of enemies, and any modification of colour which rendered her more conspicuous would often lead to her destruction and that of her offspring" (NS, p. 130). Natural selection, Wallace indicated, would tend to eliminate any variations in this direction. Conversely, any variations in color which tended to render the female less conspicuous by assimilating her to the surroundings would be favored by natural selection. Male birds, since they are not subject to such periods of enforced helplessness—and, hence, to selective pressure against (random) conspicuous color variations—would be capable of acquiring the brilliant plumage characterizing their sex only in many avian species. Wallace's argument extended to those groups of birds, including the kingfishers, trogons, and mynahs, in which the female, rather than dull, was as conspicuously colored as the male. With very few exceptions, these birds construct nests which are either domed or concealed in the hollows of trees or in burrows in the ground. The females of these species, since they are effectively hidden from predators during incubation of their eggs, are free to acquire "the same bright hues and strongly contrasted tints with which their partners are so often decorated" (NS, p. 129). Finally, in those few cases (such as the gray phalarope) in which the female is more conspicuously colored than the male, Wallace declared "it is either positively ascertained that the latter performs the duties of incubation, or there are good reasons for believing such to be the case" (NS, p. 132).

Wallace had not, at this point, altogether repudiated female choice as an influence in the evolution of certain aspects of sexual dimorphism. He did, however, relegate it to a position of subsidiary importance. The publication of Darwin's *Descent of Man* in 1871 accentuated the divergence between the two naturalists on the subject of sexual selection.[16] Darwin, in addition to arguing the case for human evolution, elaborated at length upon what he considered to be the widespread operation of male rivalry and female choice throughout the animal kingdom, including man. Wallace's review of Darwin's *Descent* emphasized his growing conviction that sexual selection was incompetent to account for the overwhelming majority of sexual differences which Darwin had documented. Even if one granted that the females of various animal species were capable of exercising a preference in the choice of mates, Wallace denied that the individual tastes of successive generations could produce any constant effect: "How are we to believe that the action of an ever varying fancy for any slight change of colour could produce and fix the definite colours and markings which actually characterize species. Successive generations of female birds choosing any little variety of colour that occurred among their suitors would necessarily lead to a speckled or piebald and unstable result, not to the beautifully definite colours and markings we see."[17] A similar objection applied to Darwin's assertion that conscious mate selection had been an important agent in determining both the racial and sexual differences of mankind. Such selection would require "the very same tastes to persist in the majority of the race during a period of long and unknown duration," an identity of tastes on the part of man's ancestors for which Wallace insisted there was simply no evidence. Moreover, as Darwin's own examples demonstrated, members of "each race admire all the characteristic features of their own race, and abhor any wide departure from it; the natural effect of which would be to keep the race true, not to favour the production of new races."[18] Only natural selection, Wallace argued, by "unerringly" selecting or rejecting variations according as they are either useful or disadvantageous, could produce fixed racial or secondary sexual characteristics. Although Wallace could assign adaptive value to only certain secondary sexual characteristics, he did not doubt the "existence of some laws of development capable of differentiating the sexes other than sexual selection."[19] Human racial differences, he suggested, were probably either adaptive themselves or correlated with useful variations (NS, pp. 178–79).

For the next two decades, Wallace continued to develop his case against sexual selection. *Darwinism* was intended, in part, to demonstrate that the varied phenomena of sexual dimorphism could be subsumed under the action of natural selection. In addition to protective coloration, Wallace declared that the need for recognition had played a decisive role in modifying the comparative coloration of the sexes. Since hybridization between members of closely related species generally results in either infertile or otherwise less fit offspring, any development which served to reduce the possibility of such crosses would be favored by natural selection. "The wonderful diversity of colour and of marking that prevails, especially in birds and insects," Wallace suggested, "may be due to the fact that one of the first needs of a new species would be, to keep separate from its nearest allies, and this could be most readily done by some easily seen external mark of difference" (D, p. 218). He emphasized that either the male or the female could be modified in color apart from the opposite sex "in the process of differentiation for the purpose of checking the intercrossing of closely allied forms" (D, p. 227, 272–73).

The fundamental disagreement between Wallace and Darwin on sexual selection emerges most clearly with respect to the phenomenon of male bird song. Darwin believed birds "to be the most aesthetic of all animals, excepting of course man, and they have nearly the same taste for the beautiful as we have."[20] The ability to sing, he maintained, is a powerful means employed by male birds "to charm the females."[21] Just as man can modify his domesticated birds by selecting those whose variations appeal to him, "so the habitual or even occasional preference by the female of the more [melodious] males would almost certainly lead to their modification ... augmented to almost any extent, compatible with the existence of the species."[22] To Wallace— for whom the discontinuity between man's higher faculties and the mental processes of the rest of the animal kingdom had become axiomatic (D, pp. 461–64)—evolutionary explanations of behavioral traits or physical characters predicated upon an aesthetic sense in lower animals were unacceptable. The imputation of aesthetic tastes to birds (and insects), he declared, was an anthropomorphism as unwarranted as that made by "writers who held that the bee was a good mathematician, and that the honeycomb was constructed throughout to satisfy its refined mathematical" sense (D, p. 336). Adroitly citing Darwin against himself, Wallace noted that the *Origin* properly ascribed the bee's instinctual hive-making ability to a gradual accumulation, by natural selection, of those variations which were conducive to the construction of the best cells with the least expenditure of labor and precious wax (D, p. 337). The song of a male bird, Wallace argued analogously, functions not to charm the female but as a call to indicate his presence. In addition to their value as a means of recognition between the two sexes of a given species, characteristic bird-calls also are signals that the pairing season has arrived. Wallace pointed out correctly that when the individuals of a species are widely scattered, such calls are of crucial importance in enabling pairing to take place as early as possible, thus reducing the period during which the potential mates are exposed to predation and other dangers in their search for each other.[23] The "clearness, loudness, and individuality of the song," Wallace concluded, "become . . . a useful character, and therefore the subject of natural selection" (D, p. 284).

But while *Darwinism* forcefully summarized his efforts to minimize the importance of sexual selection among animals, by 1890 Wallace reversed his position with respect to its efficacy in human evolution. This reversal, moreover, reflects the extent to which Wallace had now integrated his biological and social theories. Bellamy's *Looking Backward*, it is clear, provided Wallace with more than a cogent defense of socialism: it yielded an explicit mechanism (or, rather, an explicit context for that mechanism) by which human progress could be effected. In Bellamy's egalitarian future state, "sexual selection, with its tendency to preserve and transmit the better types of the race, and let the inferior types drop out, has unhindered operation." Women, free from the demands of poverty or wealth, could now choose as the fathers of their children only those men who possessed traits—"beauty, wit, eloquence, kindness, generosity, geniality, courage"

—worthy of transmission to posterity, and ensure that every "generation is sifted through a little finer mesh than the last."[24] In rejecting Malthusian variants of Social Darwinism as well as (unaided) environmental reformism, Wallace had been left with only the guidance of spiritual intelligences as a *vera causa* for further human evolution. Bellamy's work suggested another, completely naturalistic, mechanism (although one still contingent upon the presence of faculties and characteristics some of which owed their development to spiritual intelligences) whose explanatory potential Wallace fully appreciated.

The mechanism had the further advantage of providing a selective force, and hence the possibility of evolution, in an otherwise egalitarian society.[25] As a biologist, Wallace sought to demonstrate that the principle of sexual selection under socialism is scientifically defensible. In particular, he addressed himself to the objection that in an egalitarian society, with its assumed absence of the Malthusian positive checks of war, famine, and pestilence, coupled with removal of the usual economic restraints to early marriage, an inevitable overpopulation would soon plunge mankind into an ever more bitter struggle for existence. Wallace countered that delayed marriage would be enshrined as one of the fundamental conditions of Socialist society and, citing Galton, noted that the proportionate fertility of women decreased with increased age at marriage. More generally, he invoked Spencer's essay on "A Theory of Population deduced from the General Law of Animal Fertility" (1852), which suggested that the increasing complexity of civilization encouraged intelligence and self-discipline and perforce diminished fertility.[26] Finally, Wallace argued that socialism, by eradicating the dangerous conditions of labor under capitalism, would significantly lower the rate of male mortality relative to females (since men were more generally employed in dangerous occupations). The observed excess of females in the general population during the ages of most frequent marriage (from twenty to thirty-five years)—despite the statistically higher percentage of male births—would, therefore, be neutralized. In such a monogamous Socialist state women, in effect, would become the minority and female choice predicated upon an excess of males (or at least not a minority) would become biologically significant. The greater option of female celibacy (possible because of financial independence) would augment the rigor of sexual selection and, Wallace averred, ensure that those individuals "who are the least perfectly developed either mentally or physically . . . or who possessed any congenital deformity [or tendency to hereditary disease] would in hardly any case find partners, because it would be considered an offence against society to be the means of perpetuating such diseases or imperfections" (SSS, I, 524–25). Such individuals, he was careful to point out, would not be deprived of the ability to lead contented lives but only of the ability to transmit their defective traits to any offspring (SSS, II, 507).

In "Human Progress: Past and Future" (1892) Wallace elaborated upon the thesis that sexual selection under socialism afforded the sole means of effecting a permanent amelioration of human society. Although the advance in material civilization in historical times was undoubted, Wallace questioned whether there had been a corresponding advance in man's mental and moral nature (SSS, II, 493–94). Granting that "during the whole course of human history the struggle of tribe with tribe and race [with] race has inevitably caused the destruction of the weaker and the lower, leaving the stronger and the higher, whether physically or mentally stronger, to survive," he doubted whether such a process did, or ought to, operate under the conditions of modern civilization. On the one hand, such practices as the celibacy of the clergy—preventing procreation by many "to whom the rude struggle of the world was distasteful, and whose gentle natures fitted them for deeds of charity or to excel in literature or art"—and the system of inherited wealth—"which often gives to the weak and vicious an undue advantage both in the certainty of subsistence without labour, and in the greater opportunity for early marriage and leaving a numerous offspring" —have prejudicial (although opposite) effects in human evolution. On the other hand, the preservation of the weak or malformed may also be construed as interference with the course of nature (SSS, II, 496–97). Wallace noted, however, that the cultivation of sympathetic feelings "has improved us morally by the continuous development of the characteristic and crowning grace of our human, as distinguished from our animal nature" (SSS, I, 526). The fact that some who in infancy were weak or physically deformed later exhibited superior mental qualities afforded another, more practical, sanction for civilization's protection of the weak.

Wallace reiterated his concern, however, that man under the present social system was actually retarding evolution's "general advance" (SSS, II, 496). He stressed again that the widespread modern trust in education and environmental reform as the main engines of human betterment was misplaced, insofar as it was based upon the belief in the hereditary transmission "of the effects of training, of habits, and of general surroundings" (SSS, II, 505). He added, somewhat wryly, that Weismann's argument against the inheritance of acquired characteristics, whether physical or cultural, was cause for relief rather than despair: it also implied that the debauched practices of the wealthy and the sordid habits of the oppressed workers in Victorian society need not produce any permanent degradation of humanity. But Wallace was cognizant of what were commonly perceived to be the pessimistic cultural consequences of Weismannian biology. He sought to allay the fears of such leading neo-Lamarckians as the American sociologist Lester F. Ward and the geologist-biologist Joseph Le Conte that Weismann's germ plasm theory of heredity doomed to failure or ineffectuality all proposals for human betterment "except by methods which are revolting to our higher nature."[27] Far from negating the influence of education and of beautiful and healthful surroundings, Wallace asserted that human selection under socialism—because informed by an ethos of freedom and human dignity guaranteed by economic equality —necessarily entailed "that education *has* the greatest value for the improvement of mankind." Moreover, for the first time in man's history, "selection of the fittest may be ensured by more powerful and effective agencies than the destruction of the weak and the helpless" (SSS, II, 508).

Wallace considered the principle of sexual selection under socialism to be his most important contribution (ML, II, 389). Such a claim, while obviously of arguable validity given his other accomplishments, is revealing because it typifies Wallace's refusal to divorce his biology from his ethical and social thought. His attempt to construct a reformist social program rooted in, or at least consonant with, evolutionary biology takes on an

added significance given Wallace's copaternity of the principle
of natural selection. The inconsistencies, indeed contradictions,
which mark his system of social evolutionism—precisely because
they cannot be attributed to any misunderstanding of the Darwin-Wallace theory—testify all the more dramatically to the
tensions inherent in nineteenth-century attempts to wed social
policy to natural law. Drawing upon such diverse sources as
biology, spiritualism, land nationalization, socialism, and phrenology—an eclecticism which at once impressed, puzzled, or infuri-
ated his contemporaries—Wallace could scarcely have avoided
the pitfalls awaiting the too ardent synthesizer in an area as in-
tractable as that which has come to be called sociobiology. His
assertion "that the only method of advance for us, as for the
lower animals, is in some form of natural selection" (ML, II,
389), for example, obscures the discontinuity between certain
aspects of human and animal evolution he had elsewhere taken
such pains to establish. Claiming that a refurbished sexual selection "which would steadily eliminate the physically imperfect
and the socially and morally unfit" (ML, II, 267), is akin, if not
equivalent, to the "weeding-out system . . . of natural selection,
by which the animal and vegetable worlds have been improved
and developed" (SSS, I, 526), hardly clarifies the already confused terminology of nineteenth-century evolutionary biology.
This conceptual, though not moral, confusion is, finally, apparent
in Wallace's last work, *The Revolt of Democracy* (1913). There,
in exhorting the Labour party and the trade unions to continue
their battle against land monopoly and the competitive system of
industry, Wallace declared categorically that "the principle of
competition—a life and death struggle for bare existence—has
had more than a century's unbroken trial under conditions created by its upholders, *and it has absolutely failed.*"[28]

Wallace's biological socialism, ultimately, must be assessed
against the broader background of Victorian efforts to invoke
evolutionary science in behalf of causes which spanned the political spectrum. The protean guises assumed by Social Darwinism
—from conservative defenses of unregulated competition and
"rugged individualism" to the thesis of the Russian anarchist
Peter Kropotkin that mutual aid, not struggle, was the key element in the evolution of animals and humans[29]—testify more to

the fervor than to the validity of the varied political and moral claims educed from evolutionism. The affinities Wallace perceived between socialism and evolution are significant primarily because they represent yet another element in his effort to forge a holistic philosophy of man and nature. His definition of socialism as the "use by every one of his faculties for the common good, and the voluntary organization of labour for the equal benefit of all" (ML, II, 274) reflects his commitment to spiritualism and phrenology, as well as to evolution.[30] Wallace's coupling of evolution and socialism, while neither unique nor logically impeccable, is noteworthy precisely because of his eminence and scientific authority. Michael Helfand has recently argued convincingly that Wallace was the "unmentioned target" of Huxley's celebrated Romanes lecture, "Evolution and Ethics" (1893), which purported to demonstrate that social ethics could *not* be drawn from (or based upon) evolutionary biology. Ironically, "far from limiting and depoliticizing the authority of evolutionary science," Huxley's covert attack upon Wallace (and others whose social and political views he opposed)—by reintroducing the Malthusian arguments for natural selection to justify his own support of the Liberals' modified laissez-faire social policy—exposes most clearly the manner in which politics and science had become entwined in the Darwinian debates.[31]

IV   The Wonderful Century *(1898)*

An invitation to lecture on nineteenth-century science at Davos, Switzerland, in 1896 provided Wallace with an opportunity to assess the implications of the rapid advances in science and technology during the course of the past 100 years (ML, II, 228, 231). *The Wonderful Century*, which appeared two years later, is an extended critique of "those great material and intellectual achievements which especially distinguish the Nineteenth Century from any and all of its predecessors" and which have effected a fundamental transformation in the habits of European man and of those non-European cultures with whom he was coming into increasing contact.[32] Wallace's analysis of the successes and failures of the "Wonderful Century" is less a juxtaposition of commonplace Victorian eulogiums and condemnations of progress than an exploration of the apparent paradox that social, moral, and intellectual evils have themselves "grown up or persisted, in the midst of all our triumphs over natural forces, and our unprecedented growth in wealth and luxury" (WC, p. 160).

Though the consequences of scientific and technological change could hardly have failed to impress even the least observant by the century's close, *The Wonderful Century* is notable for Wallace's demonstration that both the nature and rate of scientific activity had undergone a profound transformation. Not only had the frequency of scientific discovery augmented dramatically, but such discovery had come to be characterized not by "mere improvements upon, or developments of, anything that had been done before" but by "entirely new departures, arising out of our increasing knowledge of and command over the forces of the universe" (WC, p. 3). Wallace was not, to be sure, arguing that advances in chemistry, biology, astronomy, or physics arose *de novo*. Rather, he recognized that theoretical discoveries were being translated into practical applications with such rapidity and with such far-reaching social consequences that the cumulative scientific achievements of the nineteenth century were to be compared not to those of "any preceding century or group of centuries, but rather the whole preceding epoch of human history" (WC, p. 156). This radical increase in man's ability to manipulate nature had resulted, accordingly, in developments so startling as to have been unthinkable even to the boldest scientific visionaries of the seventeenth and eighteenth centuries.

Of the inventions and practical applications of science which "are perfectly new departures," Wallace considered preeminent those which effected major changes in the customs, thoughts, and speech patterns of mankind. The railway, which revolutionized land travel, and the steam-powered ship, which revolutionized oceanic navigation, together altered irrevocably the facilities for human transport and the distribution of commodities. The electric telegraph and the telephone instituted an even greater revolution in the communication of thought and speech. Gas lighting, electric lighting, friction matches, and the use of anesthetics and antiseptics during surgery—commonplace by the century's close—had brought about equally profound changes in the conduct of ordinary life. Finally, the development of photography and of the phonograph ranked as revolutions in the reproduction and transmission of visual images and sounds as great as the invention of printing had been with respect to written symbols. In contrast to the wealth of inventions "of the first rank" of the nineteenth century, no earlier period had witnessed any equivalent prodigiousness. Indeed, all of previous human history had produced perhaps seven inventions which to Wallace merited comparison with those of the most recent decades: the steam engine, the telescope, the barometer, the printing press, the mariner's compass, and—at the dawn of history —Arabic numerals and alphabetical writing (WC, pp. 150–53).

A survey of theoretical discoveries yielded a similarly disproportionate relation between the scientific achievements of the nineteenth century (including the principle of the conservation of energy, Dalton's atomic theory, and evolution by natural selection) and those of all its predecessors combined (including Newton's law of universal gravitation, William Harvey's proof of the circulation of the blood, and Euclid's systematization of geometry) (WC, pp. 154–56). Wallace's particular selection of historically significant inventions and theories is idiosyncratic, as any such catalogue must be. He omits from consideration the mechanical clock which Lewis Mumford, for example, regards as the key invention of the modern industrial age, "the outstanding fact and the typical symbol of the machine."[33] Wallace's demonstration of the wholly exceptional character of nineteenth-century science and technology in their cultural context is cogent, nonetheless. It informs his analysis of the possible ramifications of man's radical transformation of, the environment with a perception lacking in many Victorian critiques of progress.

That these brilliant scientific and technological accomplishments had exacerbated social distress Wallace considered equally indisputable. Citing Carlyle, Ruskin, Mill, Henry George, and Frederick Harrison, he reiterated his conviction that unless a fundamental change in the organization of society were implemented, a continued degradation of the cultural and natural environment was inevitable (WC, pp. 364–65). The neglect of phrenology, mesmerism, and psychical research generally by the scientific establishment seemed further symptoms, to Wallace, of the Victorians' narrow preoccupation with the material paraphernalia of scientific advance (WC, pp. 159-212). Precisely because England had at last attained the institutionalization of scientific inquiry and innovation which Francis Bacon had envisioned more than two and a half centuries before (in the *New Atlantis*) as the means of vastly extending the possibilities of human welfare, was the Victorians' "total failure to make any adequate rational use of them" the more striking and dangerous. Wallace indicted England and the other advanced industrial nations for "expending much of their wealth and all the resources of their science, in preparation for the destruction of life, of property, and of happiness" (WC, pp. 376-77).

Internationally, scientific discoveries had been seized upon not to facilitate that peaceful intercourse between states which had been the optimistic theme of the Great Exhibition of 1851— whose Crystal Palace symbolized the beneficent potential of science and technology—but to augment the efficiency of the armies and weaponry of modern warfare. The quickening pace of military development, typified by the application of steam power to ships of war and the hitherto unrivaled "death-dealing power" of modern cannon, shells, mines, and torpedoes, seemed to Wallace cause for sadness on the part of "any thoughtful person . . . to see such skill and labour, and so much of the results of modern science, devoted to purposes of pure destruction" (WC, pp. 332-34). European imperialism, moreover, had spread not the benefits of modern culture but a ruthless competition in which the entire globe had become "but the gambling table of the six great Powers" and "millions of savage or semi-civilized peoples [were] enslaved and bled for the benefit of their new rulers" (WC, p. 337). India, which after more than a century of British rule had considerable portions of its native populations in the imperial cities of Calcutta and Bombay living "in such horribly insanitary conditions as to rival the worst plague-infested cities of Europe in the middle ages," struck Wallace as sorry but common evidence of the darker side of the much-vaunted advance of European civilization (WC, p. 340).

England's treatment of her own population, Wallace declared, was further proof that the Victorians "were morally and socially

unfit to possess and use the enormous powers for good or evil
which the rapid advance of scientific discovery had given" them
(WC, p. 340). In addition to the deplorable living conditions
of much of the working class, Wallace cited the hazardous practices of many of the new factories. Toxic chemicals such as
yellow phosphorous, employed in the production of the ignition
tips of friction matches, were handled without proper safe-
guards and caused disease and, occasionally, death among
laborers. In these and other so-called dangerous trades the
misery was "absolutely needless, since . . . all without exception
could be made entirely harmless if adequate pressure were
brought to bear upon the manufacturers" (WC, p. 355). Industrial capitalism, which Wallace claimed had failed to esti-
mate human life "as of equal value with the acquisition of
wealth by individuals," here as elsewhere militated against
the amelioration of conditions and, "with ample knowledge
of the sources of health," allowed—and even compelled—the
bulk of the population to work amid unhealthful and life-short-
ening circumstances (WC, pp. 353, 377).

These inescapable "results of the struggle for existence and
for wealth under present social conditions" were accompanied
by the advanced nations' "plunder of the earth." Unlike
the pernicious social effects of unchecked competitive capitalism,
the "reckless destruction of the stored-up products of nature"
was irretrievable. The massive exploitation of coal, petroleum,
and natural gas—in the absence of any "rational organization
of society"—resulted in great accumulations of private wealth
but only at unacceptable, and unprecedented, cost to the environment (WC, pp. 363, 367–68). Similarly, the excessive
clearing of forests in tropical countries to increase the amount
of land available for the cultivation of crops such as coffee and
tea which "give a large profit to the European planter" produced
serious damage to those countries. Rich soil (particularly on
steep hill slopes in Ceylon and India), being no longer protected by a covering of dense vegetation, "was quickly washed
away by the tropical rains, leaving great areas of bare rock or
furrowed clay, absolutely sterile, and which will probably not
regain its former fertility for hundreds, perhaps thousands, of
years" (WC, p. 371).

Whether the social evils that rendered "many of the advances of science curses instead of blessings" were necessary but temporary phenomena attending England's emergence as the first modern industrial nation, or whether they are inherent in developed capitalist societies also, are questions as controversial today as they were in 1898. Whether the movement toward socialism, which Wallace believed in process "during the last ten years, in all the chief countries of Europe as well as in America," afforded the only hope of eradicating those evils is an equally contentious, and unresolved, issue (WC, p. 378). The importance of *The Wonderful Century* lies not in posing these questions—Wallace was scarcely original in that respect—but in its clear statement that science and technology are cultural, as well as intellectual, phenomena of great complexity. Wallace's analysis of the often subtle interaction among science, technology, and society—and of the transformation of nature and of man's relationship to nature which the rapidly increasing application of science and technology was effecting—prefigures (albeit sketchily) the historical and critical scrutiny to which the cultural functions of science are increasingly subjected at present. *The Wonderful Century* is, finally, testimony to Wallace's fundamental conviction that to divorce science from its social and moral context is both logically indefensible and historically dangerous.

CHAPTER 6

Conclusion

Commenting on a review of his autobiography in 1905, Wallace wrote:

I am the one man who believes in spiritualism, phrenology, anti-vaccination, and the centrality of the earth in the universe, whose life is worth writing. Then it points out a few things I am capable of believing, but which everybody else knows to be fallacies, and compares me to Sir I. Newton writing on the prophets! Yet of course he praises my biology up to the skies—there I am wise—everywhere else I am a kind of weak, babyish idiot! It is really delightful! (ARW, pp. 449–450)

His contemporaries were variously delighted, puzzled, or repelled by Wallace's heterodox, at times apparently contradictory, eclecticism in scientific and social ideas. It often seemed simpler, especially to his scientific colleagues, to concentrate upon his undoubted biological achievements and to humor, or discreetly ignore, his other activities. Yet, as Wallace always insisted, there was a unifying force behind those diverse interests—a passionate and unyielding commitment to ensure that mankind's civilized attainments function as the agents of human betterment rather than as the causes of social malaise or destruction. In our own age, less certain of the automatic benevolence of scientific and technological advances than were the Victorians, Wallace's attempt to forge a comprehensive and meliorist conception of man and nature assumes a less eccentric and more urgent character.

It was Wallace's scientific brilliance, of course, which first established his importance to the Victorians. The discovery of natural selection—which by itself secures him a central role in the history of science—was followed by nearly five decades of

159

productive activity, during which Wallace made fundamental contributions to evolutionary biology and anthropology. Biogeography, the nature of organic variation and speciation, the origin and function of animal and plant coloration (particularly mimicry and protective resemblances), the influence of climate and glaciation in the history of life, and ethnography all are subjects which assumed their basic outlines under the imprint of Wallace's seminal and often bold theoretical innovations. To those of his peers, such as Lyell, Hooker, Huxley, and Darwin himself, who were best qualified to judge—and who would be least deceived by his persistent public deference to the author of the *Origin of Species*—Wallace's biological achievements rivaled those of Darwin.

Certain of Wallace's scientific ideas and interpretations were strongly resisted by his contemporaries. Natural selection was under constant siege throughout the latter decades of the nineteenth century, and Wallace devoted a great deal of his energies to establishing that principle as the primary mechanism of evolution. The first three decades of the twentieth century witnessed a further erosion of his and Darwin's position, and it was not until 1932, when the classic works of R. A. Fisher, Sewall Wright, and J. B. S. Haldane had been published, that the decisive arguments for natural selection were adduced and the synthetic theory of evolution established.[1] Given the nineteenth- and early twentieth-century uncertainty concerning the mechanism of inheritance, many of the debates concerning the efficacy of natural selection often turned upon fundamental misconceptions of the evolutionary process. Wallace himself failed to recognize the significance of Mendelian genetics, mistakenly regarding it as equivalent to the theory of discontinuous single-jump mutations (as opposed to small continuous variations)—associated with William Bateson and Hugo de Vries—and thus rejecting it as an erroneous alternative to natural selection.[2] Similarly, Wallace's arguments against the efficacy of natural selection in the development of certain human faculties and behavioral characteristics have lost much of their force with the acquisition of more extensive data drawn from the observation of nonhuman primates and with a more sophisticated reconstruction of the actual process of early human evolution.[3]

The role played by natural selection in the origin and perfecting of isolating mechanisms (such as sterility barriers)—a critical step in the process of speciation—fuelled one of the most intriguing debates between Wallace and Darwin (D, pp. 174–79), among others, and represents an area of evolutionary biology which is only recently receiving a definitive formulation.[4] Wallace's famous controversy with Darwin concerning the relative influence of natural selection and sexual selection betrayed another area of uncertainty in evolutionary theory, an uncertainty which persists to some degree to the present day.[5] Finally, recent evidence for continental drift has forced a revision of some aspects of Wallace's biogeographical synthesis which were predicated upon the general permanence of the major continental and oceanic features of the earth's topography.[6] The main methodological tools he forged for understanding animal and plant distribution, however, retain their validity.

Paradoxically, certain of the social and political views which brought Wallace the distinction of being "so widely known as a 'crank' and a 'faddist'" in his own day (ARW, p. 436) have become orthodox opinions in the present time. His advocacy of socialism, land nationalization, and womens' rights seems to reflect less the whims of a faddist than insights into the methods of societal reform. Other concerns, notably phrenology, anti-vaccination (WC, pp. 213–323), and the cosmic centrality of the earth and its human inhabitants, have diminished in significance or fallen into oblivion. Of Wallace's most controversial crusade—that on behalf of spiritualism—the verdict must remain suspended. However, that spiritualist convictions were central to his moral and social pronouncements is undoubted. Recent studies, furthermore, have established the influence of those convictions upon certain aspects of his scientific work, most notably those dealing with human evolution.

Wallace was writing at that period in history when, for legitimate professional reasons, the advocates of scientific naturalism were pressing strongly for an acceptance of the autonomy of science and the objectivity of its conclusions. Wallace held such a disjunction between science and its social context to be untenable. Evolutionary biology was, for him, both an explanation of natural process and one element in the effort to comprehend man as a social and ethical being. His passionate and—to many of his contemporaries—aberrant dedication to often unpopular causes, which followed from his holistic philosophy, detracted from his scientific reputation. Today, that dedication to ensure that science operate as a humane enterprise seems less a distraction than a fundamental perception of its complex cultural role.

Notes and References

Chapter One

1. Alfred Russel Wallace, *My Life: A Record of Events and Opinions* (1905; rpt. Westmead, England: Gregg International Publishers, 1969), I, 13; hereafter cited as ML.

2. John R. Durant, "Scientific Naturalism and Social Reform in the thought of Alfred Russell Wallace," *British Journal for the History of Science* 12 (1979): 33–35.

3. H. Lewis McKinney, *Wallace and Natural Selection* (New Haven and London: Yale Univ. Press, 1972), p. 5.

4. Ibid., p. 6.

5. Wilma George, *Biologist Philosopher: A Study of the Life and Writings of Alfred Russel Wallace* (London: Abelard-Schuman, 1964), p. 13.

6. Alfred Russel Wallace, *A Narrative of Travels on the Amazon and Rio Negro*, 2nd ed. (1889; rpt. New York: Dover Publications, Inc., 1972), pp. 277–78; hereafter cited as N.

7. James Marchant, *Alfred Russel Wallace: Letters and Reminiscences* (1916; rpt. New York: Arno Press, 1975), p. 45; hereafter cited as ARW.

8. ARW, p. 141; on the ambiguities inherent in the terminology employed by Wallace and Darwin see R. M. Young, "Darwin's Metaphor: Does Nature Select?" *Monist* 55 (1971): 442–503; and Edward Manier, *The Young Darwin and His Cultural Circle: A study of influences which helped shape the language and logic of the first drafts of the theory of natural selection* (Dordrecht and Boston: D. Reidel Publishing Co., 1978), pp. 5–6, 12–14, 172–86.

9. See Malcolm J. Kottler, "Alfred Russel Wallace, the Origin of Man, and Spiritualism," *Isis* 65 (1974): 174–80, for a discussion of Wallace's spiritualist activities in the 1870s.

Chapter Two

1. For a recent reconstruction of the process by which Darwin reached the theory of natural selection see Silvan S. Schweber, "The

Origin of the *Origin* Revisited," *Journal of the History of Biology* 10 (1977): 229–316.

2. Wallace, *My Life*, I, 316–20; the map is reprinted in *My Life*, I, facing p. 320.

3. Charles C. Gillispie, *Genesis and Geology: A Study in the Relations of Scientific Thought, Natural Theology, and Social Opinion in Great Britain, 1790–1850* (1951; rpt. New York: Harper Torchbooks, 1959), pp. 209–16.

4. Gillispie, *Genesis and Geology*, pp. 219–22; see also Peter J. Bowler, "Darwinism and the Argument from Design: Suggestions for a Reevaluation," *Journal of the History of Biology*, 10(1977): 29–43.

5. Baden Powell, for example—adherent of natural theology and sympathetic to evolutionary ideas—declared: "The term 'creation' indeed, especially as respects new species, seems now, by common consent, to be adopted among geologists as a mere *term of convenience,* to signify simply the fact of origination of a particular form of animal or vegetable life, without implying anything as to the *precise mode* of such origination—as simply involving the assertion that a period can be assigned at which that species appears, and before which we have no evidence of its appearance. In this sense there can be no objection to its use, but it should be carefully guarded against possible misapplication." See his *Essays on the Spirit of the Inductive Philosophy, the Unity of Worlds, and the Philosophy of Creation* (1855; rpt. Westmead, England: Gregg International, 1969), pp. 399, 476–81.

6. For a fuller discussion of Wallace's early biogeographical views see Chapter 3.

7. McKinney, *Wallace and Natural Selection*, pp. 24–26.

8. Wallace, *My Life*, I, 320–27, 331–32, 336; Wallace, *The Malay Archipelago: The Land of the Orang-utan and the Bird of Paradise; A Narrative of Travel, with Studies of Man and Nature* (London: Macmillan and Co., 1869), I, xiv. Hereafter cited as MA.

9. Alfred Russel Wallace, "On the Law Which Has Regulated the Introduction of New Species," *Annals and Magazine of Natural History* 2nd Ser., 16 (1855): 184–85; my italics.

10. Ibid., p. 186.

11. Ibid., p. 196.

12. Ernst Mayr, *Evolution and the Diversity of Life: Selected Essays* (Cambridge, Mass.: Belknap Press, 1976), p. 278.

13. David L. Hull, *Darwin and His Critics: The Reception of Darwin's Theory of Evolution by the Scientific Community* (Cambridge, Mass.: Harvard Univ. Press, 1973), p. 14.

14. Michael Ruse, "The Darwin Industry," *History of Science* 12, Pt. 1, No. 15 (1974): 54.

15. Edward Forbes, "On the Manifestation of Polarity in the Distribution of Organized Beings in Time," *Notices of the Proceedings at the Meetings of the Members of the Royal Institution* 1 (1851–1854): 428–33.

16. Wallace, "On the Law," pp. 192–93.

17. Ibid., p. 195.

18. McKinney, *Natural Selection*, p. 45.

19. Dov Ospovat, "Perfect Adaptation and Teleological Explanation: Approaches to the Problem of the History of Life in the Mid-Nineteenth Century," *Studies in History of Biology* 2 (1978): 35, 49–52, argues that the usual evolutionist-creationist dichotomy drawn between biologists in the 1850s (and later) is less meaningful than a division of biologists on the basis of whether they sought or did not seek teleological explanations in their science. Wallace's initial nonteleological, and subsequent teleological, evolutionism illustrates Ospovat's thesis in a particularly cogent manner.

20. Wallace, "On the Law," p. 187.

21. Ibid., pp. 188, 190.

22. Ibid., pp. 190–91.

23. Ibid., pp. 191–92.

24. Ibid., p. 195.

25. Ibid., p. 196.

26. Ibid., p. 190.

27. Sir Charles Lyell, *Principles of Geology: Being an Attempt to Explain the Former Changes of the Earth's Surface by Reference to Causes Now in Operation* (London: John Murray, 1832), II, 18–35.

28. Wallace, "On the Law," p. 190.

29. Alfred Russel Wallace, "Attempts at a Natural Arrangement of Birds," *Annals and Magazine of Natural History* 2nd Ser., 18 (1856): 194–96.

30. Ibid., p. 204.

31. Ibid., p. 196.

32. Ibid., pp. 196–97.

33. Ibid., pp. 207–14.

34. Ibid., pp. 198–99.

35. Alfred Russel Wallace, "Note on the Theory of Permanent and Geographical Varieties," *Zoologist* 16 (1858): 5888.

36. Ibid., p. 5887.

37. Ibid., p. 5888.

38. Ibid.

39. McKinney, *Natural Selection*, p. 30; Marchant, *Wallace*, p. 54.

40. Alfred Russel Wallace, "Notebook, 1855–1859," MS, Library of the Linnean Society of London, pp. 39–40.

41. On the role of essentialism in retarding the acceptance of evolutionary theory in the nineteenth century, see Mayr, *Evolution and the Diversity of Life*, pp. 282–83.

42. Alfred Russel Wallace, "On the Natural History of the Aru Islands," *Annals and Magazine of Natural History* 2nd Ser., 20 (1857): 478–79.

43. Ibid., pp. 480–81.

44. Ibid., p. 482.

45. Ibid., pp. 482–83.

46. Ibid., p. 483.

47. Ibid., p. 474.

48. McKinney, *Natural Selection*, pp. 131–38, claims (in a rather elaborate but not entirely convincing argument) that Wallace actually was on the nearby island of Gilolo when he recalled the work of Malthus.

49. Barbara G. Beddall, "Wallace, Darwin, and the Theory of Natural Selection: A Study in the Development of Ideas and Attitudes," *J. Hist. Biol.* 1 (1968): 299.

50. Francis Darwin, ed., *The Life and Letters of Charles Darwin: Including an Autobiographical Chapter* (New York: D. Appleton and Co., 1896), I, 473.

51. The title for the joint papers and the letter to Gray is: Charles Darwin and Alfred Russel Wallace, "On the Tendency of Species to form Varieties; and on the Perpetuation of Varieties and Species by Natural Means of Selection," *J. Linnean Soc. London* (*Zoology*) 3 (1858): 45–62; Wallace's essay occupies pp. 53–62. I have used the version reprinted in Wallace's *Natural Selection and Tropical Nature* (1891); see note 53 below. For a discussion of the complex and still ambiguous events leading to the joint publication see Beddall, "Wallace and Darwin," pp. 299–318; and McKinney, *Natural Selection*, pp. 142–46. Beddall's account—emphasizing the disappearance of the manuscript of Wallace's essay as well as the disappearance of critical letters from Wallace, Lyell, and Hooker sent to Darwin during this crucial period—is perhaps the most temperate yet forceful indictment of Darwin's, Lyell's and Hooker's handling of the joint publication and suggests, once again, that Darwin may have owed a debt (unacknowledged) to Wallace in the genesis of the *Origin* (particularly with respect to the principle of divergence).

52. Beddall, "Wallace and Darwin," p. 313.

53. Alfred Russel Wallace, "On the Tendency of Varieties to Depart Indefinitely from the Original Type," in *Natural Selection and Tropical Nature: Essays on Descriptive and Theoretical Biology* (1891; rpt. Westmead, England: Gregg International, 1969), p. 23. Hereafter cited as NS.

54. Peter J. Bowler, "Alfred Russel Wallace's Concept of Variation," *J. Hist. Med. and Allied Sciences* 31:1 (1976): 21–24.

55. Alfred Russel Wallace, *Darwinism: An Exposition of the Theory of Natural Selection with Some of Its Applications,* 1891 ed. (rpt. New York: AMS Press, 1975), pp. 410–44. Hereafter cited as D.

Chapter Three

1. Gareth Nelson, "From Candolle to Croizat: Comments on the History of Biogeography," *Journal of the History of Biology* 11 (1978): 269–86.

2. P. L. Sclater, "On the General Geographical Distribution of the Members of the Class Aves," *J. Proc. Linn. Soc. London (Zoology)* 2 (1858): 130.

3. Alfred Russel Wallace, "On the Zoological Geography of the Malay Archipelago," *J. Linn. Soc. London (Zoology)* 4 (1860): 172–84; hereafter cited as ZG.

4. Joseph Dalton Hooker, *The Botany of the Antarctic Voyage of H. M. Discovery Ships "Erebus" and "Terror" in the Years 1839–1843. II. Flora Novae-Zelandiae. Part I. Flowering Plants* (London: Lovell Reeve, 1853), p. xxi.

5. See, e.g., Darwin's letters to Lyell and Hooker in Francis Darwin, ed., *The Life and Letters of Charles Darwin* (New York: D. Appleton and Co., 1896), I, 431–36, 438–40.

6. Alfred Russel Wallace, "On the Physical Geography of the Malay Archipelago," *Jour. Royal Geographical Society* 33 (1863): 227.

7. Ibid., p. 233.

8. Ibid., pp. 226–27.

9. Charles Lyell, *Principles of Geology,* 10th ed. (London: John Murray, 1868), II, 346–53; for Darwin's reaction, see ARW, p. 132.

10. Alfred Russel Wallace, "On Some Anomalies in Zoological and Botanical Geography," *Natural History Review* 4 (1864): 111; hereafter cited as SA.

11. Morse Peckham, ed., *The "Origin of Species" by Charles Darwin: A Variorum Text* (Philadelphia: Univ. of Pennsylvania Press, 1959), pp. 562–645.

12. Lyell, *Principles of Geology,* II, 335–38.

13. Joseph Dalton Hooker, "Insular Floras," *Gardeners' Chronicle and Agricultural Gazette*, January 5, 1867, pp. 6–7, 27, 50–51, 75–76.

14. Ibid., p. 50.

15. See F. Darwin and A. C. Seward, eds., *More Letters of Charles Darwin* (New York: D. Appleton and Co., 1903), I, 486.

16. Darwin and Seward, *More Letters*, II, 7.

17. Gordon L. Davies, *The Earth In Decay: A History of British Geomorphology, 1578–1878* (New York: American Elsevier Publishing Co., 1969), pp. 267, 310.

18. W. George, *Biologist Philosopher*, p. 123.

19. Alfred Russel Wallace, *The Geographical Distribution of Animals: With a Study of the Relations of Living and Extinct Faunas as Elucidating the Past Changes of the Earth's Surface* (1876; rpt. New York and London: Hafner Publishing Co., 1962), I, vii–viii; hereafter cited as GD.

20. Wallace, GD, II, 253; see also W. George, *Biologist Philosopher*, pp. 134–35.

21. Ernst Mayr, "Wallace's Line in the Light of Recent Zoogeographic Studies," *Quarterly Review of Biology* 29 (1954): 1–14; reprinted, with minor revisions, in Mayr, *Evolution and the Diversity of Life*, pp. 626–45.

22. G. H. R. von Koenigswald, *The Evolution of Man*, rev. ed. (Ann Arbor: Univ. of Michigan Press, 1976), p. 57.

23. Alfred Russel Wallace, *Island Life: Or the Phenomena and Causes of Insular Faunas and Floras, Including a Revision and Attempted Solution of the Problem of Geological Climates*, 2nd ed., rev. (London: Macmillan and Co., 1892), pp. 73–74; hereafter cited as IL.

24. For a contemporary assessment see Joseph LeConte, *Elements of Geology*, rev. ed. (New York: D. Appleton and Co., 1882), p. 578; for the modern position see B. W. Sparks and R. G. West, *The Ice Age in Britain* (London: Methuen and Co., Ltd., 1972), pp. 26–39.

25. Jed Z. Buchwald, "Sir William Thomson," *Dictionary of Scientific Biography*, 13 (1976), 383.

26. For a discussion of Darwin's discomfiture and the general bearing of the age of the earth controversy on evolutionary biology during the 1860s and 1870s see Joe D. Burchfield, *Lord Kelvin and the Age of the Earth* (New York: Science History Publications, 1975), pp. 57–89.

27. Alfred Russel Wallace, "The Measurement of Geological Time," *Nature* 1 (1870): 399–401, 452–55.

28. Buchwald, "Thomson," p. 383.

29. Alfred Romer, "Henri Becquerel," *Dictionary of Scientific Biog-*

raphy 1 (1970): 559; Jean Wyart, "Pierre Curie," *Dictionary of Scientific Biography*, 3 (1971), 508.

Chapter Four

1. Alfred Russel Wallace, "On the Varieties of Man in the Malay Archipelago," *Transactions of the Ethnological Society of London* NS 3 (1864–1865): 211; hereafter cited as VM.

2. J. W. Burrow, *Evolution and Society: A Study in Victorian Social Theory* (1966; rpt. Cambridge: Cambridge Univ. Press, 1970), p. 131.

3. Wilma George, *Biologist Philosopher*, p. 115; for Wallace's own general reservations see ML, I, 421.

4. Alfred Russel Wallace, "The Origin of Human Races and the Antiquity of Man Deduced from the Theory of 'Natural Selection,'" *Journal of the Anthropological Society of London* 2 (1864): clxx; hereafter cited as OHR. See also Wallace, *My Life*, I, 417–18.

5. See Robert C. Bannister, *Social Darwinism: Science and Myth in Anglo-American Social Thought* (Philadelphia: Temple Univ. Press, 1979), pp. 180–200; and John S. Haller, Jr., *Outcasts from Evolution: Scientific Attitudes of Racial Inferiority, 1859–1900* (Urbana: Univ. of Illinois Press, 1971).

6. Alfred Russel Wallace, "Geological Climates and the Origin of Species," *London Quarterly Review* (American ed.) 126 (1869): 205. Wallace's response to Lyell's tenth edition of the *Principles of Geology* (1867–68) is doubly significant. On the one hand, Wallace applauds Lyell's long-awaited public endorsement of evolutionism. On the other, Wallace's announcement of his "revised" views on man parallels (though for different reasons) Lyell's expressed extreme reservations concerning natural selection and human evolution. Darwin was, understandably, disappointed with *both* Wallace and Lyell. See Michael Bartholomew, "Lyell and Evolution: An Account of Lyell's Response to the Prospect of an Evolutionary Ancestry for Man," *British Journal for the History of Science* 6 (1973): 300–303.

7. Charles Darwin, *On the Origin of Species* (1859; facsimile rpt. Cambridge, Mass.: Harvard Univ. Press, 1964), pp. 201–202.

8. Wallace, "Geological Climates," pp. 202–204.

9. Ibid., p. 205.

10. Kottler, "Alfred Russel Wallace, the Origin of Man, and Spiritualism," pp. 162, 188–92; Wallace, *Darwinism*, p. 455.

11. Several others are discussed in Chapter 2. The original title is Alfred Russel Wallace, *Contributions to the Theory of Natural Selec-*

tion (London: Macmillan, 1870); I have used the version reprinted (with alterations) in 1891: Alfred Russel Wallace, *Natural Selection and Tropical Nature: Essays on Descriptive and Theoretical Biology* (1891; rpt. Westmead, England: Gregg International, 1969); hereafter cited as NS.

12. Wallace changed the title to "The Development of Human Races under the Law of Natural Selection."

13. Alvar Ellegard, *Darwin and the General Reader: The Reception of Darwin's Theory of Evolution in the British Periodical Press, 1859–1872* (Göteborg: Elanders Boktryckeri Acktiebolag, 1958), p. 332.

14. Kottler, "Wallace and the Origin of Man," pp. 157–59.

15. Charles Darwin, *The Descent of Man, and Selection in Relation to Sex*, 2nd ed. (New York: A. L. Burt, 1874), pp. 64–65, 685–86.

16. Alfred Russel Wallace, rev. of *The Descent of Man, and Selection in Relation to Sex*, by Charles Darwin, *Academy* 2 (March 15, 1871): 179–80.

17. Darwin, *Descent of Man*, p. 70.

18. Hull, *Darwin and His Critics*, pp. 64–65.

Chapter Five

1. Alfred Russel Wallace, *On Miracles and Modern Spiritualism*, 3rd ed. (1896; rpt. New York: Arno Press, 1975), pp. 131–32; hereafter cited as MMS.

2. W. H. Brock, "William Crookes," *Dictionary of Scientific Biography*, III (New York: Charles Scribner's Sons, 1971), 475.

3. Quoted by Frank M. Turner, *Between Science and Religion: The Reaction to Scientific Naturalism in Late Victorian England* (New Haven and London: Yale Univ. Press, 1974), p. 90.

4. Kottler, "Wallace and the Origin of Man," p. 188.

5. C. G. Jung, "The Psychological Foundations of Belief in Spirits," *Proceedings of the Society for Psychical Research* 31 (1921): 75–76.

6. Turner, *Between Science and Religion*, pp. 78–82, 88.

7. Alfred Russel Wallace, "How to Nationalize the Land: A Radical Solution of the Irish Land Problem," *Contemporary Review* 38 (1880): 716–36; *Land Nationalisation: Its Necessity and Its Aims*, 4th ed. (London: Swan Sonnenschein and Co., Lim., 1906); hereafter cited as LN.

8. Peter d'A. Jones, *The Christian Socialist Revival, 1877–1914:*

Religion, Class, and Social Conscience in Late–Victorian England (Princeton: Princeton Univ. Press, 1968), p. 55.

9. Robert M. Young, " 'Non-Scientific' Factors in the Darwinian Debate," *Actes, XIIe Congrès Internationale d'Histoire des Sciences, 1968* 8 (Paris, 1971): p. 223.

10. Alfred Russel Wallace, *Studies Scientific and Social* (London: Macmillan and Co., 1900), I, 509; hereafter cited as SSS.

11. George W. Stocking, Jr., "Lamarckianism in American Social Science: 1890–1915," *Journal of the History of Ideas* 23 (1962): 239–56.

12. Gloria Robinson, "August Weismann," *Dictionary of Scientific Biography*, 14 (New York: Charles Scribner's Sons, 1976), pp. 234–37.

13. Darwin, *Origin of Species*, pp. 88–89.

14. "Mimicry, and Other Protective Resemblances Among Animals," *Westminster Review*, NS 32 (1867): 1–43; it is reprinted in NS, pp. 34–90; "On Birds' Nests and Their Plumage" was read to the British Association for the Advancement of Science, meeting in Dundee in 1867; a more complete analysis was published the next year as "A Theory of Birds' Nests" and is reprinted under the title "A Theory of Birds' Nests, Showing the Relation of Certain Differences of Colour in Female Birds to Their Mode of Nidification" in NS, pp. 118–40.

15. Henry Walter Bates, "Contributions to an Insect Fauna of the Amazon Valley," *Transactions of the Linnean Society of London* 23 (1862): 512–13; Darwin wrote a favorable (but unsigned) review of Bates' article in the *Natural History Review* 3 (1863): 219–24; for Wallace's endorsement see his "On the Phenomena of Variation and Geographical Distribution as illustrated by the *Papilionidae* of the Malayan Region," *Transactions of the Linnean Society of London* 25 (1865): 19.

16. With the possible exception of the origin of man, no issue divided Wallace and Darwin as sharply as sexual selection; see, e.g., ARW, pp. 175–78, 181–90, 210–14, 245–48 and D, pp. 282–88, 294–96. The questions of female choice, the origin of human racial characteristics, and the precise relation between natural selection and sexual selection are complex and continue to be a source of biological controversy. Edward B. Poulton, *The Colours of Animals: Their Meaning and Use, Especially Considered in the Case of Insects* (London: Kegan Paul, Trench, Trübner, and Co., 1890), is an important contemporary account. For recent analyses see Michael T. Ghiselin, *The Triumph of the Darwinian Method* (Berkeley and Los Angeles: Univ. of California Press, 1969), pp. 214–31, and Bernard Campbell, ed., *Sexual Selection and the Descent of Man, 1871–1971* (London:

Heinemann, 1972). Malcolm Jay Kottler has recently offered a detailed analysis of the richness and flexibility of both Wallace's and Darwin's positions, with an extensive citation of the important correspondence between the two during the late 1860s and early 1870s; see his "Darwin, Wallace, and the Origin of Sexual Dimorphism," *Proceedings of the American Philosophical Society* 124 (1980): 203–26.

17. Wallace, rev. of *Descent of Man*, p. 182.

18. Ibid., pp. 179–80.

19. Ibid., p. 182.

20. Darwin, *Descent of Man*, pp. 407–408.

21. Ibid., p. 421.

22. Ibid., p. 479.

23. Ernst Mayr, "Sexual Selection and Natural Selection," in *Sexual Selection and the Descent of Man, 1871–1971*, ed. B. Campbell, p. 96.

24. Edward Bellamy, *Looking Backward: 2000–1887* (1888; rpt. New York: The Modern Library, 1942), p. 218.

25. R. M. Young, " 'Non-Scientific' Factors," p. 224, is not entirely correct in stating that "socialism and nineteenth-century evolutionism were always very uneasy bedfellows, and in the conflict between them Wallace chose socialism." As we have seen, sexual selection provided a mechanism by which socialism and evolution could be made compatible: Wallace did not have to choose between the two.

26. SSS, I, 521–23; on the ambiguities inherent in Spencer's treatment of population, and evolutionary theory generally, see Bannister, *Social Darwinism*, pp. 41–56.

27. SSS, II, 508; on the disturbed reaction to Weismann's "neo-Darwinism" see Bannister, *Social Darwinism*, pp. 138–41.

28. Alfred Russel Wallace, *The Revolt of Democracy* (London: Cassell and Co., Ltd., 1913), pp. 76–77.

29. Kropotkin presented his views, in reply to Huxley's influential essay "The Struggle for Existence" (1888), in a series of articles which appeared in the *Nineteenth Century* between 1890 and 1896; they were collected and published in 1902 as *Mutual Aid*. I have used Peter Kropotkin, *Mutual Aid: A Factor in Evolution*, ed. from 3rd ed. (1914) by Paul Avrich (New York: New York Univ. Press, 1972).

30. Roger Smith, "Alfred Russel Wallace: Philosophy of Nature and Man," *British Journal for the History of Science* 6 (1972): 195–96.

31. Michael S. Helfand, "T. H. Huxley's 'Evolution and Ethics': The Politics of Evolution and the Evolution of Politics," *Victorian Studies* 20 (1977): 176–77.

32. Alfred Russel Wallace, *The Wonderful Century: Its Successes*

and Its Failures (1898; rpt. Westmead, England: Gregg International Publishers Ltd., 1970), p. v; hereafter cited as WC.

33. Lewis Mumford, *Technics and Civilization* (1934; rpt. New York: Harcourt, Brace and World, Inc., 1963), p. 14.

Chapter Six

1. George C. Williams, *Adaptation and Natural Selection: A Critique of Some Current Evolutionary Thought* (1966; rpt. Princeton: Princeton University Press, 1974), p. 3.

2. Wilma George, "The Reaction of A. R. Wallace to the Work of Gregor Mendel," *Folia Mendeliana* 6 (1971): 175–76.

3. G. G. Simpson, "The Evolutionary Concept of Man," in B. Campbell, ed., *Sexual Selection*, pp. 31–32.

4. E. Mayr, "Darwin, Wallace, and the Origin of Isolating Mechanisms," in Mayr, *Evolution and the Diversity of Life*, pp. 129–34.

5. E. Mayr, "Sexual Selection and Natural Selection," in B. Campbell, ed., *Sexual Selection*, pp. 87–104.

6. G. Nelson, "From Candolle to Croizat," pp. 295–96.

Selected Bibliography

PRIMARY SOURCES

1. Books

Australasia. Edited and extended by Alfred Russel Wallace. With an Ethnological Appendix by A. H. Keane. London: Edward Stanford, 1879.

Bad Times: An Essay on the Present Depression of Trade, Tracing It to Its Sources in Enormous Foreign Loans, Excessive War Expenditure, the Increase of Speculation and Millionaires, and the Depopulation of the Rural Districts; with Suggested Remedies. London: Macmillan and Co., 1885.

Contributions to the Theory of Natural Selection: A Series of Essays. London: Macmillan and Co., 1870.

Darwinism: An Exposition of the Theory of Natural Selection with Some of Its Applications. London: Macmillan and Co., 1889.

The Depression of Trade: Its Causes and Its Remedies. Edinburgh: Co-operative Printing Co., Ltd., 1886.

The Geographical Distribution of Animals: With a Study of the Relations of Living and Extinct Faunas as Elucidating the Past Changes of the Earth's Surface. 2 vols. London: Macmillan and Co., 1876; rpt. New York and London: Hafner Publishing Co., 1962.

Is Mars Habitable?: A Critical Examination of Professor Percival Lowell's Book "Mars and Its Canals," with an Alternative Explanation. London: Macmillan and Co., 1907.

Island Life: Or the Phenomena and Causes of Insular Faunas and Floras, Including a Revision and Attempted Solution of the Problem of Geological Climates. London: Macmillan and Co., 1880; 2nd and rev. ed., 1892.

Land Nationalisation: Its Necessity and Its Aims, Being a Comparison of the System of Landlord and Tenant with That of Occupying Ownership in Their Influence on the Well-Being of the People. London: Swan Sonnenschein and Co., Lim., 1882; 4th ed., 1906.

The Malay Archipelago: The Land of the Orang-Utan, and the Bird of Paradise; A Narrative of Travel, with Studies of Man and Nature. 2 vols. London: Macmillan and Co., 1869.

Man's Place in the Universe: A Study of the Results of Scientific Research in Relation to the Unity or Plurality of Worlds. London: Chapman and Hall, 1903.

Miracles and Modern Spiritualism. London: James Burns, 1875; rev. ed., with chapters on apparitions and phantasms. London: George Redway, 1896; rpt. Arno Press: New York, 1975.

My Life: A Record of Events and Opinions. 2 vols. London: Chapman and Hall, Ltd., 1905; rpt. Westmead, England: Gregg International Publishers Limited, 1969.

A Narrative of Travels on the Amazon and Rio Negro: With an Account of the Native Tribes, and Observations on the Climate, Geology, and Natural History of the Amazon Valley. London: Reeve and Co., 1853; 2nd ed., London: Ward, Lock and Co., 1889; rpt. New York: Dover Publications, Inc., 1972.

Natural Selection and Tropical Nature: Essays on Descriptive and Theoretical Biology. London: Macmillan and Co., 1891; rpt. Westmead, England: Gregg International Publishers Limited, 1969.

Palm Trees of the Amazon and Their Uses. London: J. Van Voorst, 1853.

The Revolt of Democracy: With the Life Story of the Author by James Marchant. London: Cassell and Co., Ltd., 1913.

Social Environment and Moral Progress. New York: Cassell and Company, 1913.

Studies Scientific and Social. 2 vols. London: Macmillan and Co., 1900.

Tropical Nature and Other Essays. London: Macmillan and Co., 1878.

The Wonderful Century: Its Successes and Its Failures. London: Swan Sonnenschein and Co., Limd., 1898; rpt. Westmead, England: Gregg International Publishers Limited, 1970.

The World of Life: A Manifestation of Creative Power, Directive Mind and Ultimate Purpose. London: Chapman and Hall, 1910.

MARCHANT, JAMES. *Alfred Russel Wallace: Letters and Reminiscences.* New York and London: Harper and Brothers Publishers, 1916; rpt. New York: Arno Press, 1975.

2. Periodical Literature

"Attempts at a Natural Arrangement of Birds." *Annals and Magazine of Natural History* 2nd ser., 18 (1856): 193–216.

"The Colours of Animals and Plants." *Macmillan's Magazine* 36 (1877): 384–408, 464–71.

"Darwinism *versus* Wallaceism." *Contemporary Review* 94 (1908): 716–17.

"Geological Climates and the Origin of Species." *Quarterly Review* 126 (1869): 359–94.

"How to Nationalize the Land: A Radical Solution of the Irish Land Problem." *Contemporary Review* 38 (1880): 716–36.

"Human Progress: Past and Future." *Arena* 5, No. 26 (1892): 145–59.

"Human Selection." *Fortnightly Review* NS 48 (1890): 325–37.

"Lamarck *versus* Weismann." *Nature* 40 (1889): 619–20.

"Letter from MR. WALLACE concerning the Geographical Distribution of Birds." *Ibis* 1 (1859): 449–54.

"The Measurement of Geological Time." *Nature* 1 (1870): 399–401, 452–55.

"The Method of Organic Evolution." *Fortnightly Review* NS 57 (1895): 211–24, 435–45.

"Mimicry, and Other Protective Resemblances Among Animals," *Westminster Review*, NS 32 (1867): 1–43.

"Note on the Theory of Permanent and Geographical Varieties." *Zoologist* 16 (1858): 5887–88.

"On Some Anomalies in Zoological and Botanical Geography." *Natural History Review* 4 (1864): 111–23.

"On the Law which has regulated the Introduction of New Species." *Annals and Magazine of Natural History* 2nd ser., 16 (1855): 184–96.

"On the Natural History of the Aru Islands." *Annals and Magazine of Natural History* 2nd ser., 20 (1857): 473–85.

"On the Phenomena of Variation and Geographical Distribution as illustrated by the *Papilionidae* of the Malayan Region." *Transactions of the Linnean Society of London* 25 (1865): 1–71, plates I–VIII.

"On the Physical Geography of the Malay Archipelago." *Journal of the Royal Geographical Society* 33 (1863): 217–34.

"On the Tendency of Varieties to Depart Indefinitely from the Original Type." *Journal of the Linnean Society of London, Zoology* 3 (1858): 53–62.

"On the Varieties of Man in the Malay Archipelago." *Transactions of the Ethnological Society of London* NS 3 (1864–1865): 196–215.

"On the Zoological Geography of the Malay Archipelago." *Journal of the Linnean Society of London, Zoology* 4 (1860): 172–84.

"The Origin of Human Races and the Antiquity of Man Deduced

from the Theory of 'Natural Selection.'" *Journal of the Anthropological Society of London* 2 (1864): clviii–clxx.

"The Problem of Utility: Are Specific Characters Always or Generally Useful?" *Journal of the Linnean Society of London, Zoology* 25 (1896): 481–96.

"Remarks on the Rev. S. Haughton's Paper on the Bee's Cell, and on the Origin of Species." *Annals and Magazine of Natural History* 3rd Ser., 12 (1863): 303–309.

Rev. of *The Descent of Man, and Selection in Relation to Sex,* by Charles Darwin. *Academy* 2 (1871): 177–83.

NOTE: There exists no authoritative bibliography of Wallace's more than 400 books, articles, and reviews. The most useful, but still incomplete and often inaccurate, is Marchant (1916), pp. 477–86.

SECONDARY SOURCES

BANNISTER, ROBERT C. *Social Darwinism: Science and Myth in Anglo-American Social Thought.* Philadelphia: Temple Univ. Press, 1979. A comprehensive and important study of the ideological uses of evolutionary biology.

BEDDALL, BARBARA G. "Wallace, Darwin, and the Theory of Natural Selection: A Study in the Development of Ideas and Attitudes." *Journal of the History of Biology* 1 (1968): 261–323. A major reinterpretation of certain aspects of the discovery of natural selection. Clarifies Wallace's crucial role in the steps leading to the 1858 joint publication.

———. "Wallace, Darwin, and Edward Blyth: Further Notes on the Development of Evolution Theory." *Journal of the History of Biology* 5 (1972): 153–58. Emphasizes the significance of Wallace's 1855 paper.

BOWLER, PETER J. "Alfred Russell Wallace's Concepts of Variation." *Journal of the History of Medicine and Allied Sciences* 31 (1976): 17–29. Argues that Wallace's ideas on the precise relation between natural selection and the variability of species were not as fully developed as Darwin's at the time of the joint publication.

BRACKMAN, ARNOLD C. *A Delicate Arrangement: The Strange Case of Charles Darwin and Alfred Russel Wallace.* New York: Times Books, 1980. Although exaggerated and historically naive, Brackman's book does demonstrate that Darwin, Hooker, and Lyell acted with less than complete rectitude in preparing the joint publication of 1858.

BROOKS, JOHN LANGDON. "Extinction and the Origin of Organic Diversity." *Connecticut Academy of Arts and Sciences, Transactions* 44 (1972): 19–56. Argues that Darwin incorporated—without acknowledgment—certain points from Wallace's 1855 and 1858 essays in the preparation of the *Origin*.

BURROW, J. W. *Evolution and Society: A Study in Victorian Social Theory.* Cambridge: Cambridge Univ. Press, 1966. Somewhat perverse, but a provocative and important analysis.

CAMPBELL, BERNARD, ed. *Sexual Selection and the Descent of Man: 1871–1971.* London: Heinemann, 1972. Essays on the contemporary status of sexual selection as an agent in human evolution.

DARWIN, CHARLES. *On the Origin of Species,* 1859; facsimile rpt. Cambridge, Mass.: Harvard Univ. Press, 1964.

————. *The Descent of Man, and Selection in Relation to Sex,* 2nd ed. New York: A. L. Burt, 1874.

DURANT, JOHN R. "Scientific Naturalism and Social Reform in the Thought of Alfred Russel Wallace." *British Journal for the History of Science* 12 (1979): 31–58. One of the very few studies focusing on Wallace's social and political thought.

EISELEY, LOREN. *Darwin's Century: Evolution and the Men Who Discovered It.* New York: Doubleday and Company, Inc., 1958. Idiosyncratic, but some perceptive comments on Wallace's contributions.

ELLEGARD, ALVAR. *Darwin and the General Reader: The Reception of Darwin's Theory of Evolution in the British Periodical Press, 1859–1872.* Göteborg: Elanders Boktryckeri Actiebolag, 1958. Indispensable analysis of the initial British response to Darwin's and Wallace's theory.

FICHMAN, MARTIN. "Wallace: Zoogeography and the Problem of Land Bridges." *Journal of the History of Biology* 10 (1977): 45–63.

GEORGE, WILMA. *Biologist Philosopher: A Study of the Life and Writings of Alfred Russell Wallace.* London: Abelard-Schuman, 1964. Reliable. Emphasizes Wallace's scientific contributions. Despite the title, little attempt is made to analyze fully, or integrate, his philosophical and sociopolitical concerns.

————. "The Reaction of A. R. Wallace to the Work of Gregor Mendel." *Folia Mendeliana* No. 6 (1971): 173–77. Brief but useful analysis of Wallace's failure to recognize the importance of Mendelian inheritance.

GHISELIN, MICHAEL T. *The Triumph of the Darwinian Method.* Berkeley and Los Angeles: Univ. of California Press, 1969. Controversial but significant study, with some astute comments on methodological differences in the approaches of Darwin and Wallace.

GILLISPIE, CHARLES COULSTON. *Genesis and Geology: A Study in the Relations of Scientific Thought, Natural Theology, and Social Opinion in Great Britain, 1790–1850,* 1951; rpt. New York: Harper and Row, 1959. Useful background for assessing the initial reception accorded Darwin's and Wallace's theory in Britain.

GLICK, THOMAS F., ed. *The Comparative Reception of Darwinism.* Austin and London: Univ. of Texas Press, 1974. Essays providing a cross-cultural perspective.

HEFFERNAN, WILLIAM C. "The Singularity of Our Inhabited World: William Whewell and A. R. Wallace in Dissent." *Journal of the History of Ideas* 39 (1978): 81–100. Analyzes the broader significance of Wallace's role in the late Victorian debate on the plurality of inhabited worlds.

HELFAND, MICHAEL S. "T. H. Huxley's 'Evolution and Ethics': The Politics of Evolution and the Evolution of Politics." *Victorian Studies* 20 (1977): 159–77. Argues that Wallace's socialism was the unmentioned target of Huxley's essay.

HENDERSON, GERALD. "Alfred Russel Wallace: His Role and Influence in Nineteenth Century Evolutionary Thought." Diss. University of Pennsylvania 1958.

HERBERT, SANDRA. "The Place of Man in the Development of Darwin's Theory of Transmutation": "Part I: To July 1837." *Journal of the History of Biology* 7 (1974): 217–58; "Part II." *J. Hist. Biol.* 10 (1977): 155–227. Valuable contribution to the current reassessment of the history of evolutionary biology.

HIMMELFARB, GERTRUDE. *Darwin and the Darwinian Revolution,* 1959; rpt. New York: W. W. Norton and Co., 1968. An often-cited but often-misguided study which must be used with caution.

HULL, DAVID L. *Darwin and His Critics: The Reception of Darwin's Theory of Evolution by the Scientific Community.* Cambridge, Mass.: Harvard Univ. Press, 1973. A collection of major contemporary reviews of the *Origin* which is useful for interpreting Wallace's impact also.

JUNG, C. G. "The Psychological Foundations of Belief in Spirits." *Proceedings of the Society for Psychical Research* 31 (1921):

75–93. Some perceptive comments on Wallace's spiritualism.

KOTTLER, MALCOLM JAY. "Alfred Russel Wallace, the Origin of Man, and Spiritualism." *Isis* 65 (1974): 145–92. Major study of the relationship between Wallace's commitment to spiritualism and his evolutionary theory.

————. "Darwin, Wallace, and the Origin of Sexual Dimorphism." *Proceedings of the American Philosophical Society* 124 (1980): 203–26. Detailed study of the different positions of Wallace and Darwin with respect to the relative roles of sexual selection and natural selection.

LAWRENCE, ELWOOD P. *Henry George in the British Isles*. East Lansing: The Michigan State Univ. Press, 1957. Clarifies the distinctions between the reform proposals of Wallace's Land Nationalization Society, the Socialists, George's "single-tax" program, and the Labour party.

LIMOGES, CAMILLE. *La sélection naturelle: Etude sur la première constitution d'un concept (1837–1859)*. Paris: Presses Universitaires de France, 1970. Important study.

LINNEAN SOCIETY OF LONDON. *The Darwin-Wallace Celebration Held on Thursday, 1st July, 1908, by the Linnean Society of London*. London: Printed for the Linnean Society, Burlington House, 1908. Includes the famous but not entirely trustworthy reminiscenses of Wallace and Hooker a half-century after the 1858 joint publication.

LOEWENBERG, BERT JAMES. *Darwin, Wallace and the Theory of Natural Selection, including the Linnean Society Papers*. Cambridge, Mass.: Arlington Books, 1959.

MANIER, EDWARD. *The Young Darwin and His Cultural Circle: A Study of Influences Which Helped Shape the Language and Logic of the First Drafts of the Theory of Natural Selection*. Dordrecht and Boston: D. Reidel Publishing Co., 1978. As the title implies, but also suggestive for analyzing Wallace's methodology and metaphors.

MAYR, ERNST. "Wallace's Line in the Light of Recent Zoogeographic Studies." *Quarterly Review of Biology* 29 (1954): 1–14; reprinted, with minor revisions, in Mayr, *Evolution and the Diversity of Life: Selected Essays*. Cambridge, Mass.: Belknap Press, 1976, pp. 626–45.

————. "Isolation as an Evolutionary Factor." *Proceedings of the American Philosophical Society* 103 (1959): 221–30. Discusses Wallace's and Darwin's views on geographic isolation and speciation.

————. "The Nature of the Darwinian Revolution." *Science* 176 (1971): 981–89; revised and reprinted in Mayr, *Evolution and the Diversity of Life,* pp. 277–96. Useful survey of the varied elements comprising the complex "Darwinian Revolution."

McKinney, H. Lewis. *Wallace and Natural Selection.* New Haven and London: Yale Univ. Press, 1972. A major analysis of Wallace's scientific development to 1858. Emphasizes Wallace's influence on Lyell and Darwin.

————. "Alfred Russel Wallace." *Dictionary of Scientific Biography* 14 (1976), 133–40. Balanced biographical sketch.

Nelson, Gareth. "From Candolle to Croizat: Comments on the History of Biogeography." *Journal of the History of Biology* 11 (1978): 269–305. An important re-examination, biased against the Wallace-Darwin tradition.

Osborn, Henry Fairfield. "Alfred Russel Wallace." *Popular Science Monthly* 83 (1913): 523–37. Laudatory obituary.

Ospovat, Dov. "Perfect Adapation and Teleological Explanation: Approaches to the Problem of the History of Life in the Mid-Nineteenth Century." *Studies in History of Biology* 2 (1978): 35–56. Questions the utility of the traditional evolutionist-creationist dichotomy drawn between mid-century biologists.

Poulton, E. B. "Alfred Russel Wallace, 1823–1913." *Proceedings of the Royal Society of London* Ser. B, 95, (1923–1924): i–xxxv. Lengthy obituary by an important contemporary.

Ruse, Michael. *The Darwinian Revolution.* Chicago and London: Univ. of Chicago Press, 1979.

Schweber, Silvan S. "The Origin of the *Origin* Revisited." *Journal of the History of Biology* 10 (1977): 229–316. Focuses on Darwin but suggestive for analyzing Wallace's evolutionary synthesis.

Smith, Roger. "Alfred Russel Wallace: Philosophy of Nature and Man." *British Journal for the History of Science* 6 (1972): 177–99. One of the best of the few recent critical analyses of the interdependence of the diverse aspects of Wallace's thought. Marred only by Smith's failure to distinguish between Wallace's 1864 essay on the origin of man and its altered 1870 version.

Turner, Frank M. *Between Science and Religion: The Reaction to Scientific Naturalism in Late Victorian England.* New Haven and London: Yale Univ. Press, 1974. Situates Wallace within the broader context of the Victorian malaise with respect to extreme scientific naturalism.

Vorzimmer, Peter J. *Charles Darwin: The Years of Controversy.*

The 'Origin of Species' and Its Critics, 1859–1882. Philadelphia: Temple Univ. Press, 1970. Treats the initial opposition engendered by the theory of natural selection, focusing on variation. Includes a chapter on the differences between Wallace and Darwin.

WILLIAMS-ELLIS, AMABEL. Darwin's Moon: A Biography of Alfred Russel Wallace. London and Glasgow: Blackie, 1966. Anecdotal and superficial. A gossipy account—primarily of Wallace's travels —rather than a biography.

WILSON, LEONARD G. Charles Lyell, The Years to 1841: The Revolution in Geology. New Haven: Yale Univ. Press, 1972.

WRIGHT, CHAUNCEY. Rev. of Contributions to the Theory of Natural Selection, by Alfred Russel Wallace. North American Review 111 (1870): 282–311. A hostile, but telling, methodological critique.

YOUNG, ROBERT M. "Malthus and the Evolutionists: The Common Context of Biological and Social Theory." Past and Present No. 43 (1969): pp. 109–45. A significant contribution to the re-evaluation of the cultural context of Victorian evolutionary biology.

————. " 'Non-Scientific' Factors in the Darwinian Debate." Actes, XIIe Congrès Internationale d'Histoire des Sciences, 1968 8 (Paris, 1971): 221–26. Incorrectly argues that Wallace was forced to choose between socialism and evolutionism.

Index